STRATEGIC INTERACTION

by
ERVING GOFFMAN

Strategic Interaction

University of Pennsylvania Publications in
Conduct and Communication

ERVING GOFFMAN AND DELL HYMES, FOUNDING EDITORS
Dell Hymes, Gillian Sankoff, and Henry Glassie, General Editors

Strategic
Interaction

Erving Goffman

upp

UNIVERSITY OF PENNSYLVANIA PRESS

PHILADELPHIA

For financial support in writing these essays I am grateful to the Institute of International Studies, University of California at Berkeley, and to the Center for International Affairs, Harvard University, where I was able to work on the volume as a Fellow during 1966–1967.

Contents

Preface

My ultimate interest is to develop the study of face-to-face interaction as a naturally bounded, analytically coherent field —a sub-area of sociology.

To do this one must come to terms with the fact that the central concepts in the area are ambiguous, and the bordering fields marked off badly.

A good example of the difficulty is the term communication. This concept has been one of the most promising in the social sciences. For the last fifty years every generation of students has applied it with new hope to new areas. But although communication has often been offered as the medicine, it has seldom produced a cure. That to which the term obviously and centrally applies—socially organized channels for transceiving information—has received very little systematic ethnographic attention. And the discovery that communication could be used broadly to refer to what happens when individuals come together has been almost disastrous: communications between persons in each other's presence is indeed a form of face-to-face interaction or conduct, but face-to-face conduct itself is never merely and not always a form of communication.

The broadening of the concept communication, then, has been a doubtful service; communication systems themselves have been neglected and the field of face-to-face interaction embraced by arms that are too small for it. The two papers in this volume attempt to go in the other direction. Drawing on some recent work done in the public reaches of game theory, they examine what is broadly thought of as communicative behavior and consider the senses in which this can be analyzed in noncommunication terms within a game perspective.

This volume thus deals with the calculative, gamelike aspects of mutual dealings—what will be called *strategic interaction*. By examining strategic interaction in its own terms, we can become clear about what it is; being clear, we will be better equipped to set it in its special place when looking at face-to-face interaction. By seeing that communication is of limited analytical significance in strategic interaction, we can prepare ourselves to find its limited place in the naturalistic study of face-to-face conduct. On both counts we will be further on the way to segregating those concerns which draw illustrations from the realm of immediate conduct (and in turn illuminate it) but draw their basic analytical concepts from other sources.

E. G.

January 1969

Expression Games:

An Analysis of Doubts at Play

Expression Games:
An Analysis of Doubts at Play[1]

In pursuit of their interests, parties of all kinds must deal with and through individuals, both individuals who appear to help and individuals who appear to hinder. In these dealings, parties—or rather persons who manage them—must orient to the capacities which these individuals are seen to have and to the conditions which bear upon their exercise, such as innate human propensities, culture-bound beliefs, social norms, the market value of labor, and so forth. To orient to these capacities is to come to conclusions, well founded or not, concerning them; and to come to these conclusions is to have assumptions about the fundamental nature of the sorts of persons dealt with.

These assumptions about human nature, however, are not easy to uncover because they can be as deeply taken for granted by the student as by those he studies. And so an appeal is made to extraordinary situations wherein the student can stumble into awareness. For example, during periods of marked social change, when individuals acquire rights or lose them, attention is directed to properties of individuals which will soon become defined as simply human and taken

[1] A preliminary statement appears in *Strategic Interaction and Conflict*, ed. K. Archibald (Berkeley, Calif.: Institute of International Studies, 1966), pp. 198ff. I am grateful to Dr. Archibald for a great number of suggestions which I have incorporated freely into the text without acknowledgment.

for granted.[2] During occasions when new industries and technologies are developed, the physical and physiological details usually taken as given can become a matter of concern, with consequent clarification of the assumptions and conceptions we have of what individuals are. Thus, in designing aircraft for flight above 15,000 feet it is necessary to consider human needs for oxygen and warmth; in designing aircrafts as big as Howard Hughes' flying boat it is necessary to consider the limits of human strength, since motorized assists will be necessary in design of the controls; in designing large, fast planes it is necessary to consider the limits of one person's capacity to process information, there being a point where the addition of more instruments will require the addition of an extra pilot; and in designing spacecraft, of course, it is necessary to consider not merely human physiological functions, but also the individual's capacity as a material object.

In this paper I want to explore one general human capacity in terms of the conceptions we have of its physical and social limits: the individual's capacity to acquire, reveal, and conceal information. The perspective here is that of an organizationally committed observer who needs information from another person. I will draw upon the popular literature on intelligence and espionage for illustration, for no party seems more concerned than an intelligence organization about the capacity we will consider, and more likely to bring assumptions to the surface for us. Special attention will be given to occasions when the informing individual is in the immediate presence of the party collecting the information.

I ASSUMPTIONS

1. Individuals, like other objects in this world, affect the surrounding environment in a manner congruent with their

---

[2] See, for example, R. Bendix, *Work and Authority in Industry* (New York: John Wiley & Sons, 1956).

own actions and properties. Their mere presence produces signs and marks. Individuals, in brief, exude expressions.

The information contained in the expressions which an individual exudes has special features. It necessarily concerns the source of expression and cannot solely be about some absent object. It is not discursive in the sense of providing an extended argument, but rather pertains to the general relationship of that individual to what is transpiring. (Thus, meaning is very much bound to context.) The generating of expression, and hence making its information available, is not an official end of the action, but (at least ostensibly) only a side effect. Here, then, is *expressed information*. It is the kind I will mainly be concerned with.

Any contact which a party has with an individual, whether face-to-face or mediated by devices such as the mails, will give the party access to expression. Immediacy, then, does not mark the analytical boundary for the study of expression. Nonetheless, face-to-face interaction has a special place because whenever an individual can be observed directly a multitude of good sources of expressed information become available. For example, appearance and manner can provide information about sex, age, social class, occupation, competencies, and intent.

2. There are means, then, some quite standard, through which the individual *expresses* information. But of course there is an important complication to be added to this picture. Individuals offer more than expressions; they also offer communications. I here refer to a special type of instrumental activity, the use of language or language-like signs to *transmit* information—this being communication in the narrow sense of that much-abused term. The intentional transmission of information, as far as we know, is largely a human process arising when the signs mean to the sender what they mean to the recipient, and when the controlling and openly avowed (if not actual) purpose of the sender is to impart correct, adequate information to the recipient, the signs being institu-

5

tionalized for this purpose. Typically the signs employed are of the generative kind, able to support an enormous number of different statements; typically discursive strips of information are producible; typically the message is somewhat free of context and its subject matter is not at all restricted to the sender. I shall speak here of *communicated information* (or transmitted information or a message), and the process through which this information is conveyed, *communication* or *transmission*.[3]

Communicated information can be described by means of a few principal terms derived from a few principal issues. Start with the central notion of an observer, now in the role of an interrogator, putting a question to a subject.

One issue will be the relation of the subject's answer to the facts. This involves two matters. First, the answer can be said to possess a particular degree of "repleteness." At one extreme, it may appear to cover all the facts, making the interrogator feel that it is unnecessary to continue seeking information on the question. At the other extreme, the subject may reply that he has no relevant information to offer. Second, answers can vary as to their "correctness," according to how well they somehow fit, match, or correspond to the facts.

Another issue will be the relation of what is said to what is known by the sayer. Three matters are involved here. The first is that no-information replies can be of several varieties: "Don't know"; "Know but won't tell"; and "Not telling, nor telling whether I could tell." The second point is that when

---

[3] See the parallel arguments by Tom Burns in *Discovery*, October 1964, p. 32. The stricture I am placing on the term communication some students would only place on language and its substitutes. Here see C. Hockett, "Logical Considerations in the Study of Animal Communication," in W. Lanyon and T. Tavolga, eds., *Animal Sounds and Communications* (Washington: Intelligencer, 1960), pp. 392–420. Students of animal behavior generally accept a broad view of communication and the notion that conspecifics communicate to one another. Behavior is cited which seems to have as its main remaining function its value as a source of information for animals in observational range of it. See S. Altmann, ed., *Social Communication among Primates* (Chicago: University of Chicago Press, 1967).

the subject does not reply negatively he still may reply with varying degrees of disclosure of what he thinks might be relevant. This is the question of "frankness" or "candor." The third point is that the answer given by the subject may be one he believes and would give to himself, or one he disbelieves and would not give were he asking the question of himself. The issue here is that of "honesty" or "self-belief." [4] Note, there is some likelihood that self-believed statements will be correct and self-disbelieved statements incorrect, but of course the other combination of these statuses is possible.[5]

It need only be added that everyday language tends to be ambiguous regarding the various relationships that have been reviewed, and here common usage might best be avoided. For example, when the term *truth* is employed, it is often difficult to know whether the reference is to any self-believed statement, any correct statement, or any self-believed correct statement. Similarly, the phrase "full reply" fails to distinguish between repleteness and candor.

3. The behavioral and technical process through which information is *communicated*, like all other human activities, will naturally exude expressions, and indeed that is why communication will have to be considered in this paper. The least the communicating can express is that the sender has the capacity and apparently the willingness to communicate.

---

[4] As we will later see, the issues of repleteness, correctness, candor, and self-belief are often complicated by considerations of a higher order involving one individual's relation to another individual's relation to a statement. Does the hearer believe that the speaker believes what he tells him? If not, does the hearer make it apparent that this is the case? The point, of course, is that regardless of whether the speaker himself believes in what he is saying, it is important in his coping with the hearer to know whether or not the latter really believes what he gives the appearance of believing regarding the relation of the speaker to his own statements.

[5] When the question the interrogator puts to the subject itself refers to the status of the reply, as in, "Are you answering me with a statement that you yourself believe," then two interesting possibilities arise. An affirmative answer collapses the two statuses, correct-incorrect and self-believed–self-disbelieved, into one. A negative answer, *viz,* "No, I am not replying with a statement I myself believe," gives rise to Epimenides' paradox.

Further, for those familiar with the sender, the style of a mediated communication is likely to be sufficiently expressive to tell them whether or not the claimed sender is sending it.[6] (The standard example here is the use that banks make of check signatures: semantic content communicates whose account is involved; style expresses whether or not this person himself actually signed and therefore authorized the check.)

---

[6] Authentication through the expressive aspect of communication is illustrated in the available literature on espionage, for example, R. Seth, *Anatomy of Spying* (New York: Dutton, 1963), pp. 138–139:

During this training time he was required to operate transmission schedules with the actual operators in the communications center who would receive his schedules from the field. This was not only to give him practice in operating under field conditions, but allegedly gave his contacts in the communications center an opportunity of getting to know his Morse "handwriting." It was believed at the time, though there is some difference of opinion among the experts, that the rhythm a man uses in sending Morse is as distinctive as his handwriting. If his set and his codes were captured by the enemy and the enemy decided to use them in attempts to hoodwink S.O.E., the operators in the communications center were expected to know at once what had happened by the difference in the "handwriting."

See also E. Cookridge, *Inside S.O.E.* (London: Arthur Barker, 1966), p. 84:

Usually the signals from an agent in the field were received at the scheduled time by the same FANY telegraphist. Thus the operator had his distinct "godmother" at the W/T station, somewhere in a stately home in Oxfordshire or Gloucestershire. As every operator has an individual touch on the Morse key, she would get to know his 'fist' and, if the touch was very different, could detect an imposter.

Similarly, G. Perrault, *The Secrets of D-Day* (London: Barker, Ltd., 1964), p. 124:

Hans Schmidt, for instance, had been sending messages for three years under the supervision of the British officers who had caught and then turned him . . .
Schmidt's survival was entirely due to the fact that a tape-recording made by him was kept in the Abwehr files. Each radio operator has his own particular rhythm and touch—his 'signature.' By comparing a spy's transmission with the specimen tape previously recorded, the Abwehr was assured that he himself was sending the message. It would have been useless for the English to have put Hans Schmidt quietly away and had someone else operate his transmitter.

Mechanical devices for encoding messages not only exude information about the encoder, but also leave their own stamp on the message. See, for example, D. Crown, "Landmarks in Typewriting Identification," *Journal of Criminal Law and Police Science*, 58 (1957), 105–111.

8

In addition to expressing who it is that is communicating, transmission also expresses the location of the communicator, thus giving rise to a standard problem of agents who use shortwave transmitters.[7]

Just as the process of communicating information itself expresses information, so also a corpus of communicated signs has expressive aspects. Discursive statements seem inevitably to manifest a style of some kind, and can never apparently be entirely free of "egocentric particulars" and other context-tied meanings.[8] Even a written text examined in terms of the semantic meaning of the sentences can be examined for expression that derives from the way a given meaning is styled and patterned, as when *Izvestia* and *Pravda* are read by our intelligence people "symptomatically," for what the Russians do not know they are exuding through the print.[9] Indeed, the very sense of a message depends on our telling whether it is conveyed, for example, seriously, or sarcastically or tentatively, or as an indirect quotation, and in face-to-face communication this "framing" information typically derives from paralinguistic cues such as intonation, facial gestures, and the like—cues that have an expressive, not semantic, character.

We can say, then, that as a source of information the individual exudes expressions and transmits communications, but that in the latter case the party seeking information will still

---

[7] Location by signal-source is of course common in regard to nonsymbolic activity too, as when submarines are located by the sound of their propellers. Common, too, is this function of sound signals in the animal world:

The clicking sounds of the juveniles of some species with rapidly repeated clicklike pulses having wide frequency spectrum, are among the easiest sounds to locate in space accurately and quickly and are less likely to be masked by environmental sounds than pure tones might be—all factors consistent with the function of alerting and guiding the parents to a lost or endangered infant. [P. Marler, "Communication in Monkeys and Apes," ch. 16, p. 568, in *Primate Behavior*, ed. I. DeVore (New York: Holt, Rinehart & Winston, 1965)]

[8] A point recently argued by H. Garfinkel and H. Sacks in their work on conversational settings.

[9] A useful illustration of this sort of textual analysis is available in A. George, *Propaganda Analysis* (White Plains: Row, Peterson, 1959).

have to attend to expressions, lest he will not know how to take what he is told. Thus we have two protagonists, observer and subject. When words are involved, we can speak of an interrogator and an informant.

4. All organisms after their fashion make use of information collected from the immediate environment so as to respond effectively to what is going on around them and to what is likely to occur. In the case of the lower organisms, no appreciable intelligence is involved and one can only say that in consequence of natural selection information is gathered and used "in effect." With higher organisms, especially man, instinct is not sufficient and self-conscious intentional efforts are made to acquire information from local events, with the purpose in mind of using this knowledge to deal with these events. One may speak here of a party assessing its situation, the assessment involving both the collection of information and its use in helping to arrive at decisions.

Just as it can be assumed that it is in the interests of the observer to acquire information from a subject, so it is in the interests of the subject to appreciate that this is occurring and to control and manage the information the observer obtains; for in this way the subject can influence in his own favor responses to a situation which includes himself. Further, it can be assumed that the subject can achieve this end by means of a special capacity—the capacity to inhibit and fabricate expression.

There will be situations where an observer is dependent on what he can learn from a subject, there being no sufficient alternate sources of information, and the subject will be oriented to frustrate this assessment or facilitate it under difficult circumstances. Under these conditions gamelike considerations develop even though very serious matters may be at stake. A contest over assessment occurs. Information becomes strategic and expression games occur. I argue that this situation is so general and so central that by looking at such games

10

and at the various restrictions and limitations placed upon them, we can begin to learn about important assumptions and beliefs concerning the nature of individuals.

II THE BASIC MOVES

1. Inanimate objects can certainly be said to be indifferent to whether or not they are under observation. Presumably whatever state the object is in, it will persist in this state whether observed or not—the exception that is famous at the subatomic level being of no concern to us. It is also the case that there will be occasions when animate subjects including the highest will be, for all practical purposes, unoriented to and unconcerned about being under observation—at least observation by particular observers with particular interests —whether this is due to actual ignorance that such observation is occurring or dim appreciation associated with quite genuine indifference. In any case, the observer can feel that he does not have to correct his observations for the possible masking that the subject might engage in because of this observation, that he can, in fact, take what he observes at face value, as ingenuous uncalculating expression or candid communication; and in taking this view the observer, at times, can be quite justified.

A subject's observable behavior that is unoriented to the assessment an observer might be making of it can be called an *unwitting move*. Such activity is at once part of the expression game and not part of the game and requires a paradoxical title.

2. The term *naïve move* can be used to refer to the assessment an observer makes of a subject when the observer believes that the subject can be taken as he appears, that is, that he is involved in an unwitting move. The subject is assumed to be in clear text, readable by anyone with the technical competence to see. This is the second move in expression

games. It is restricted to observers and is not available to informants. And it is a move that does not distinguish between animate and inanimate subjects.

The point here is that the individual, as a source of strategic information, may be no different whatsoever from other aspects of the scene, and at such times might even be referred to by the same term we use to designate other informing aspects of the environment. Moreover, whenever the individual himself functions as a source of information, other aspects of the scene in which he makes his appearance are very likely to serve also; in fact, observers tend to engage in continuous cross-referencing of various parts of the scene, including the individuals in it.

3. The term *control move* will be used to refer to the intentional effort of an informant to produce expressions that he thinks will improve his situation if they are gleaned by the observer. This is the third move in expression games. Note that through the process of natural selection, lower organisms very clearly come to make this move but of course only "in effect," albeit with so much effective ingenuity as to provide advanced suggestion in the art of disguise. Among humans, the process is self-conscious and calculated—although habit can bring spontaneity—this constituting a principal way in which the human gamester differs from the lesser kind. The subject appreciates that his environment will create an impression on the observer, and so attempts to set the stage beforehand. Aware that his actions, expressions, and words will provide information to the observer, the subject incorporates into the initial phases of this activity a consideration of the informing aspects of its later phases, so that the definition of the situation he eventually provides for the observer hopefully will be one he feels from the beginning would be profitable to evoke. To this end, the subject turns on himself and from the point of view of the observer perceives his own activity in order to exert control over it. He follows G. H. Mead's dictum and "takes the attitude" of the observer, but

only insofar as the observer is engaged in observing him and ready to make decisions on this basis, and only long enough and deep enough to learn from this perspective what might be the best way to control the response of the person who will make it; the observer "takes" the viewpoint of the subject, but he does not "identify" his interests with it.[10] The subject thus tends to make use of the observer's use of his behavior before the observer has a chance to do so. He engages in impression management.

A control move, we should see, is made with reference to what is already part of the game, namely, the second move; it is made relative to a world that has already been generated by the game.

And note that although verbal reticence and use of self-disbelieved statements are favorite control moves, the process of control can be quite well analyzed without reference to communication at all. What is essentially involved is not communication but rather a set of tricky ways of sympathetically taking the other into consideration as someone who assesses the environment and might profitably be led into a wrong assessment (or a right one despite his suspicions, ignorance, or incompetence). The various processes of control do not strike at the observer's capacity to receive messages, but at something more general, his ability to read expressions. Thus, when the subject employs verbal means to convey information about his intended course of action, the observer —if he is properly to judge the significance of these communications—will have to attend to the expressive aspects of the transmission as a check upon semantic content. Similarly, in trying to conceal while communicating, the subject, too, will have to attend to his own expressive behavior. A message, then, functions merely as one further aspect of the situation which must be examined carefully and controlled carefully

---

[10] R. Turner, "Role-taking, Role Standpoint, and Reference-Group Behavior," *American Journal of Sociology*, LXI (1956), 319.

because of the contest of assessment between the subject and the observer.

Look now at some standard control moves. Among lower organisms a fairly clear distinction can be made between camouflage, whereby an organism assimilates itself in appearance to the inanimate surrounding environment, and misrepresentation, this taking two forms, the simulation of another species and the simulation of threatening gestures.[11] (Interestingly, although predators do not threaten their prey with fake gestures, they do employ camouflage and misrepresentation in precisely the same way as do prey.) Among humans a distinction may be useful among the arts of: 1) concealment or cover, 2) accentuated revealment, and 3) misrepresentation. Of these three, concealment or cover seems the most important. Consider its varieties.

A common covering move is found in the act of open secrecy and privacy, whereby the subject keeps observers from perceiving something but makes no effort to prevent their perceiving that they are being kept in the dark. Perhaps even more common is covert concealment, as when subjects on the same team communicate to one another by means of furtive code.[12] Covert concealment, of course, implies a mask or camouflage of some kind.[13] (When the mask hides the purpose for

---

[11] See H. Cott, *Adaptive Coloration on Animals* (London, 1940); A. Portman, *Animal Camouflage* (Ann Arbor: University of Michigan Press, 1959); R. Caillois, *The Mask of Medusa* (New York: Potter, 1960).

[12] Agents arranging a meeting over the phone may use a contact procedure that conceals the place and time within a statement of plans that both know is not meant to be followed. For eavesdroppers who do not suspect, this is covert concealment for those who do, overt concealment.

[13] C. Felix, *The Spy and His Masters* (London: Secker and Warburg, (1963), pp. 23–26, argues a slightly different division, recommending what he claims is the usage among intelligence people: overt secret operations are ones where the sort of thing that is going on is admitted, but the details are kept a secret; covert operations are ones that are carried on under a disguise or cover of some kind; clandestine operations are ones totally hidden from view in any guise. Criminal actions usually have both a covert and clandestine character, depending on the phase of the operation. Check forging, an exception, is wholly covert. See E. Lemert, "An Isolation and Closure Theory of Naive Check Forgery," *Journal of Criminal Law, Criminology and Police Science*, 44 (1953), 298.

being present, it is sometimes called a "cover reason"; when an organized activity, a "cover operation"; when a social or personal identity, simply a "cover." [14]) Another covering move is to postpone as long as possible either making a decision or beginning the course of action which is called for by a decision already made. (It is thus that the military may wait as long as possible before finally deciding on a point of invasion, or a trainer may wait until his jockey is in the paddock before telling him whether to "shoot" or "run stiff." [15]) Also, there is the tack of minimizing the number of persons who are entrusted with strategic information and the period of time during which they possess it, on the assumption that every individual privy to a situation is a threat to security. Further, the subject (under the influence of game theory) can select a move on the basis of a randomizing device over which he has no control, thus ensuring that the observer will not be able to dope out the decision beforehand—and sometimes it will be in the subject's interests to make sure that the observer knows this strategy is being used.

If the subject has not decided on a course of action yet, he can feign that he has, or he can feign that he hasn't when he has. Also, he can feint a course of action when he has not started his actual course or has started a different one. Note that here *feinting* refers to faked courses of action, as when the military employ a "cover target" for purposes of misdirecting the counterefforts of the enemy, whereas *feigning*

---

[14] Cover is qualified as to light (shallow) or deep, depending apparently on its secureness, based on such matters as number of persons in on the secret, thoroughness of the disguise, etc. Here, see Felix, *op. cit.*, p. 77, and S. De Gramont, *The Secret War* (New York: Dell, 1963), p. 137. Of course in practice, depth alone is not enough in the management of one's cover. As Felix (*ibid.*, p. 72) suggests:

> To be too precise in a cover story qualitatively increases the chances of repudiation of the story; to be too detailed increases those chances qualitatively. To speak out too fast is to show your hand before you know all you can about what your opponent is holding in his and to tell all in one bleat eliminates our chances to improvise as the situation develops.

[15] M. Scott, "A Note on the Place of Truth," *Berkeley Journal of Sociology*, 8 (1963), 36–38.

refers to beliefs, attitudes, and preferences misrepresented strategically. A nonmilitary example might be cited:

> Florence, Italy—Italy's leading designers may soon learn to their sorrow that noisy applause doesn't mean a jingling cash register.
>
> Of the 50 American buyers at the Pitti Palace show of spring fashions, several admitted off the record that they never clap for the haute couture creations they like best. They don't want their competitors to know what they will order.
>
> At the same time these buyers confessed, they applauded enthusiastically for sportswear, boutique items and gowns that they wouldn't consider featuring in their own stores.[16]

A subject, in addition to feigning and feinting, can provide the observer with "accounts" and "explanations," these being verbal techniques for radically altering the assessment that the observer would otherwise make. And here, of course, we clearly see that individuals have a special quality as gamesmen that sharply distinguishes them from other elements in expression games. When, for example, a mock-up air base is perceived to be made of canvas and two-by-fours, it must accept its discrediting, but when a dissembler is caught out, he will often have a brief opportunity to employ wit in creating the kind of explanation and excuse that will allay suspicions. A hiding place discovered by the observer remains passively exposed; a person caught in *flagrante delicto* can sometimes talk his way out of the situation.

It will be apparent that the techniques of impression management so far considered all involve the introduction of some kind of obfuscation, some kind of "noise." [17] But, of

---

[16] WNS, in Sunday *Call-Chronicle*, Allentown, Pennsylvania, February 3, 1963.

[17] Natural selection achieves the same result. In "reply" to the capacity of predators to locate their prey through sound, a covering noise is sometimes developed:

> When a sharp-shinned hawk, *Accipiter striatus*, or sparrow hawk, *Falco sparverius*, approaches a flock of bushtit, *Psaltriparus minimus*, these tiny birds unite in a shrill quavering trill for as long as 2 minutes, and Joseph

course, as suggested, there will be times when noise is the last thing that the subject wants to create. At times he will find it expedient to reveal as unmistakably as possible what he has done or intends doing, or his resolve, resources, information, and so forth—a tack recommended to the strong because of the value of deterrence, and illustrated by situations in which heads of state publicize military accomplishments usually kept secret. Yet here expression games are no less involved.

Further, an expression game may involve contestants who have a shared purpose, or a partially shared one, for such players can still be involved in the necessity of reading another's expression and ensuring that their own is correctly read. In the usual case the contest is between observer and subject; in "games of coordination," we can think of the observer and subject teamed together in a contest against nature or against the score achieved by other such pairs, as in matchpoint duplicate bridge.

4. Three basic moves have been considered so far: the unwitting move, whereby the subject acts mindlessly relative to impression management; the naïve move, whereby the observer draws information from what he takes to be an unwitting move; the covering move, through which the subject attempts to influence the conclusions that the observer comes to. A fourth basic move may be considered. The observer, suspecting that what he might have treated as an unwitting move is actually or possibly an obfuscation or misrepresentation, suspecting that what appears to be ingenuous fact could be shot through and through with a gamesman's manipulation and design, suspecting this, he can attempt to crack, pierce, penetrate, and otherwise get behind the apparent

---

Grinnell (1905) ["Call notes of the bush-tit," *Condor* 5, 85–87] who described this shrill *confusion chorus* said that the remarkable thing about it is that it is absolutely impossible to locate any single one of the birds by it. [N. Collias, "An Ecological and Functional Classification of Animal Sounds," in Lanyon and Tavolga, *op. cit.*, p. 372]

facts in order to uncover the real ones. The observer performs an *uncovering move.*

One standard uncovering move is to perform an examination of some kind. Some examinations focus on the track that the subject leaves, his spoor, as it were. Others involve some form of interviewing and require his presence. These latter differ among themselves widely according to the strategic conditions under which they are conducted. There are covert interviews which the observer attempts to conduct so delicately that the subject (the observer hopes) remains unaware that information gathering is going on, being thus entrapped into an unwitting move. There are medical examinations which attempt to check up on the subject's claim and appearance of illness (or wellness) by employing schooled diagnosticians. There are courtroom testimonials where special sanctions are available for making it costly to communicate self-disbelieved statements. There are inquisitions with supernatural means of determining whether or not the subject is trying to conceal anything. And of course there are interrogations where the observer has some official warrant for putting a long series of questions to the subject and the latter has some reason to give the appearance, valid or not, that he desires to cooperate with the questioner in elicitation of information. (There are many standard uncovering devices used by the interrogator, including everything from the monitoring of the subject's autonomic responses as a check upon overt statements, to the so-called "trick question"—this involving the putting of a question whose answer seems to be, but isn't, one that could be figured out by a respondent who didn't know the answer but wanted to give the appearance that he did.)

Another major device is that of spying. The observer can attempt to penetrate locked or hidden containers and record the content thereof. He can attempt to monitor the subject when the latter feels he is not subject to this kind of surveillance and need not cloak his behavior.

An interesting aspect of many uncovering techniques derives from the human nature of the player himself, pointing to the strategic vulnerabilities of individuals *qua* subjects.

As suggested, in assessing a subject's situation, the observer must mobilize his understanding of subjects of that kind and, insofar as possible, put himself in the subject's shoes in order to predict the subject's action. When the observer's subject is an inanimate object, projecting its possible line of activity can be a limited thing, limited in fact to the special experience the observer may have had with such subjects, and to such special knowledge as he may acquire about them. When the subject is a person like the observer, especially one from the observer's own cultural world, then the "doping out" function becomes more intimate. An important aspect of the human subject's situation is his motivation and intent, and these have the special character that, although they can never be directly accessible to anyone except him who mentally possesses them, nonetheless, they can be sympathetically appreciated by an observer in a fuller way than he can appreciate anything about something that is inanimate. Motives and intent constitute a basic part of the subject's situation, ensuring that he is something that can be totally misunderstood or understood all too well. A basic means, then, for getting behind the cover that the subject apparently maintains is to discover through empathy his motive and intent; conversely, a basic reason for uncovering a subject is to discover his motive and intent.

5. Just as subjects can be aware that they must mask their actions and words, so they can appreciate that the controls they employ may be suspected, the covers they use penetrated, and that it may be necessary to attempt to meet this attack by countering actions, namely, *counter-uncovering moves*. Here, I think, is the final move in expression games.[18] It can be a very effective one. The very tendency of the ob-

---

[18] Only in exemplary cases can the effort of the observer to counter this counter be usefully distinguished from a simple uncovering move.

server to suspect the subject and try to seek out means of piercing the veil means that the observer will shift his reliance to the very special signs upon which he puts great weight; and if these signs can be discovered and faked by the subject, the latter will find himself dealing, in effect, with an ingenuous opponent. The best advantage for the subject is to give the observer a false sense of having an advantage— this being the very heart of the "short con."

Counter-uncovering moves are often made in regard to particular social events that would otherwise be revealing. Sorensen, in his memoirs of the Kennedy years, provides the following example: to forestall suspicion among the Press that a crisis had occurred in regard to offensive missiles in Cuba, the members of the National Security Council, coming together for a crucial meeting in the Oval Room of the White House, arrived at different times and entered through different gates.[19] During the same tense period, Kennedy apparently maintained his normal schedule of appointments to avoid arousing suspicions.[20] Another example is the spotty alibi: the subject senses that the interrogator may suspect a pat and perfect alibi, one that is conclusive and detailed, one that is just the kind of alibi someone wanting to be sure of having one would have; the subject therefore intentionally presents an incomplete alibi, doing so even when the real facts allow him to present a better one. Similarly, the subject can engineer a discrediting of his own disguise, a blowing of his own cover, so that what is revealed (sometimes through what is called a "reserve story"), will be uncritically taken to constitute the actual reality, the more so if the disclosure is severely unflattering.[21]

Counter-uncovering moves can, of course, strike at the basic sources of information associated with all subjects.

<hr>

[19] T. Sorensen, *Kennedy* (New York: Harper & Row, 1965), p. 63.

[20] *Ibid.*, p. 686.

[21] See for example, O. Pinto, *Spy Catcher* (New York: Berkeley Publishing Corporation, 1952), pp. 41–42, "The Story within a Story"; and Perrault, *op. cit.*, p. 116.

First, there is physiological expression, the symptom equipment of the subject himself. (The central assumption here is that "emotional expressions," especially ones associated with facial display, somehow portray or betray a subject's inward feelings, attitudes, desires, and so forth.) Margaret Mead, discussing Soviet conduct, provides an illustration of the countering of this expression:

> With this requirement, that all behavior be controlled and directed toward Party goals, goes the requirement that the Party member treat himself as a tool to carry out the wishes of the Party, but that he be at all times a conscious tool, voluntarily submitting himself to the discipline of the Party. And the discipline must be minute and detailed, over himself and over his every movement. So as an informant reports an encounter with a Soviet professor in Berlin, who told her that he smoked a pipe "because while smoking a pipe the face does not reveal much." Then he added:
> "See, this we learned during the Soviet period. Before the revolution we used to say: 'The eyes are the mirror of the soul.' The eyes can lie—and how. You can express with your eyes a devoted attention which, in reality, you are not feeling. You can express serenity or surprise. I often watch my face in the mirror before going to meetings and demonstrations and . . . I was suddenly aware that even with a memory of disappointment, my lips became closed. That is why by smoking a heavy pipe, you are sure of yourself. Through the heaviness of the pipe, the lips become deformed and cannot react spontaneously." [22]

The implication here is that the subject must appreciate that his protestations might not be believed and that they will be checked out against facial expressions for incongruities, and so facial display must be controlled lest it give the show away. A still deeper game with symptom equipment is possible. For example, those who run mission centers and try

---

[22] M. Mead, *Soviet Attitudes toward Authority* (New York: McGraw-Hill, 1951), pp. 65–66.

to keep them dry sometimes employ a "checker" to ensure that alcoholics going upstairs to sleep, and of apparently sober mien, do not, in fact, have liquor on their breath. A guest who does may have to learn to counter this uncovering move:

> The sniffers at the desk are good at catching you. Some men fool them by using those little bottles of stuff that kill your breath instantly. I carry a tube of toothpaste with me inside my coat and just about half a block away from the [Mission] Center front door I put a coupla squirts of that in my mouth, mush it around and walk right up to the desk and get my key—they can't tell a thing.[23]

Experts can carry this sort of work one step further. A soldier, for example, who wants to be excused from duty on account of sickness faces the fact that medical officers know the complex of symptoms a claimant should be manifesting if his claims are justified, and he, the claimant, either does not know how he should be appearing or, knowing this, does not know how to manufacture the appearance. During the last war, however, the game of illness claim was raised a level by British Special Operations. Simulated packets of German foodstuffs were distributed to German soldiers. These contained instruction booklets and phials of chemicals which equipped their possessors to simulate syndromes of the great diseases so convincingly that some German medical officers apparently ceased to trust any signs.[24]

Next to consider are "identity tags," namely officially recognized seals which bond an individual to his biography. Passports, for example, illustrate the class of certificates which are designed to establish someone's claim to something through marking of some kind that is openly given the function of being unforgeable. These documents constitute a kind of open challenge, an admission that an expression game is being

---

[23] Reported in J. Wiseman, "Making the Loop: The Institutional Cycle of Alcoholics," Ph.D. dissertation, University of California, Department of Sociology, 1968, p. 378.

[24] E. Butler, *Amateur Agent* (London: Harrap, 1963), p. 132.

played and that through identification devices the person who would misrepresent himself will be defeated. It is then no wonder that subjects sometimes accept the challenge and see if they can beat the documenter at his avowed game. It is more interesting to note that to accomplish this sort of move extensive technical facilities may be organized to specialize in the work of counter-uncovering:

> I decided that the very first job to be done was the organization of a plant for documentation—a fascinating, meticulous, deadly business, indeed. It was obvious that any spies or saboteurs O.S.S. placed behind enemy lines would have short shrift unless they had perfect passports, workers' identification papers, ration books, money, letters and the myriad little documents which served to confirm their assumed status. These are the little things upon which the very life of the agent depended.
>
> Nor was reproduction of enemy documents ordinary. All such documents had the most secret security built into them, just so no one could imitate them. Even the paper on which they were printed or engraved was made of special fibers, not to mention invisible inks, trick watermarks and special chemicals incorporated into the paper so the Japanese or German counter-intelligence could instantly expose a forged or spurious document.[25]

Identity tags are the most institutionalized of the expressions here being considered. Behind these are informal ones, such as a mental record of biographically relevant facts, for example, names of sibs, past employers, towns of residence,

---

[25] S. Lovell, *Of Spies and Stratagems* (Englewood Cliffs: Prentice-Hall, 1963), p. 23. Another example is the plant assembled in Germany for counterfeiting five pound notes during the last war. Here, see A. Pirie, *Operation Bernhard* (New York: Grove Press, 1963). Incidentally, there have been other types of specialized establishments equipped to serve in the contest of expression, for example, Prussian spymaster William Stieber's Green House used in Berlin at the turn of the century as a place equipped to seduce into blackmailability European diplomats and agents of various tastes in pleasure. See A. Ind, *A History of Modern Espionage* (London: Hodder and Stoughton, 1965), p. 49. Apparently Heydrich also used a version ("Salon Kitty") of such a house in the last war. (*Ibid.*, p. 267.)

schools attended, regiments fought in, and so forth. More informal still is the run of information—including local geographical lore—which any resident of a claimed domicile is likely to possess. In brief, local cognitive orientation is required. Cookridge provides a statement:

> The first condition for an agent in the field merely to survive, let alone to fulfill any of his tasks, was to have perfect knowledge of the required language. This meant much more than being a fluent speaker. He had to behave as a "native" to avoid attention. When one thinks of all the little points of knowledge and experience one possesses purely from being brought up or living in a country—to be familiar with a nursery rhyme, a proverb, or a song; to know the names of some famous sportsmen or film stars; to show an awareness of the common attitudes of the community which reflect, amongst other things, class and regional differences, whether related to food and wine, religion and customs—all this is entailed in the attempt at blending into the background. And, of course, the agent, a stranger arriving suddenly from nowhere, had to have a region, class, family, occupation and full identity of his own, which he could pass off as a lifetime's experience, or people would notice something odd and conscious about him.[26]

In addition to cognitive matters, there are behavioral ones. The subject will have to have some concern about the many little patterns of personal and social behavior which could distinguish him by age, sex, race, class, region, and nationality from the person he claims to be.[27]

Another source of expression consists of minor items of milieu which adhere to the person or to his effects. A subject misrepresenting himself will therefore be advised to make

---

[26] Cookridge, op. cit., p. 62.

[27] See for example, P. Monat, Spy in the U.S. (New York: Berkeley Medallion Book, 1965), p. 191. There is in fact a sizable lore regarding what might be called culture-pattern slips. Thus: "The British once uncovered a double agent in Egypt because he forgot to urinate in the approved fashion of the native men, with his knees slightly bent." See R. Alcorn, No Bugles for Spies (New York: Popular Library, 1962), p. 11.

scenic corrections. This is particularly apparent in the intelligence practice of "authentication," that is, ensuring that
minor parts of the scene have been attended to and faked,
in addition to the major ones:

> Even a hastily trained agent, or an agent who was not
> trained at all, had a fair chance of success if he was properly
> authenticated. Authentication was the third step in the OSS
> process, and it is an art as intricate as that of the watchmaker,
> as precise as that of the eye surgeon.
>
> An agent traveling in an occupied country must wear clothes
> of the occupied country. The slightest variation will give him
> away. An American laundry and cleaning mark, for example,
> would be tantamount to a death warrant; yet those cleaning
> marks are impossible to remove. They had to be cut out and
> patched over, an improvisation which was suspicious and not
> entirely effective. Other give-aways are: the manner in which
> buttons are sewn on—The Americans do it in criss-cross, Euro-
> peans in parallel; the lining—European linings are full; the
> adjustment buckles—in Europe they bear the mark of the coun-
> try of origin; suspender buttons—no matter what European
> country they come from, they bear the imprint, "Elegant," "For
> Gentlemen," or "Mode de Paris."
>
> And not only the clothes had to be checked. A man in Ger-
> many, or France, or Greece, who pulled unconsciously from
> his pocket an English match, an American cigarette, or a knife
> which was not made in Europe, was unconsciously, but very
> clearly, saying to anyone who watched him, "I am a spy." An
> agent's clothes, and the everyday articles he carried in his
> pocket, were just as important as his knowledge of the language
> and the various passes which he possessed.[28]

Interestingly, once an agent suspects that he will be in-
spected for minor cues of authentication, he can provide some

---

[28] S. Alsop and T. Braden, *Sub Rosa: The OSS and American Espionage*
(New York: Harcourt, Brace & World, 1964), pp. 41–42. A lore has developed here, too. Thus, Alcorn (*op. cit.*, p. 54) suggests that in providing agents
with notes newly arrived from the Bank of France it was necessary not only
to age them but to pin-prick them, since French bank clerks pin bundles of
bills when counting them.

that might not otherwise have been sought. He can fabricate just those little leavings of the self that shrewd observers might use as a check upon official but false presentations:

> Security agents of all countries know from experience that a respectable occupation of a man may be just a cover for illicit activities, and the physical genuineness of a passport does not always prove conclusively that it belongs by right to the bearer. That is why, when security agencies begin to entertain doubts about the identity of a foreigner in their country, they try to obtain collateral data which might shed light on him. The security officers first look for such evidence in the apartment of the suspect. They secretly obtain entry into his rooms (unlawfully, of course, but a practice in every country) and examine his personal belongings, letters, and the contents of the pockets in his wardrobe.
>
> Knowing this, the NKVD intelligence has devised the so-called "secret exhibition" which in a few known cases has proved most effective. This device consists of a series of clues planted by the Soviet agent in his own apartment in such a way that if the clues catch the eye of the secret intruders they will give them proof that the foreigner is indeed the person he represents himself to be. For instance, if the operative lives under a Canadian passport, among his belongings will be scattered a couple of old postcards mailed to his address in Montreal and duly stamped by the post office, a seasonal suburban railway ticket, a public library card from his home town issued in his name, a membership card from a Canadian club, an original telegram delivered to his store. The mere sight of a tube of Canadian toothpaste or of accessories used only in Canada or the United States, an invoice from a Canadian department store in the operative's vest pocket, or a crumpled bus ticket will impress investigators as objective proof.[29]

A concluding note about counter-uncovering moves in particular and the other kinds of moves in general. Expression

---

[29] A. Orlov, *Handbook of Intelligence and Guerrilla Warfare* (Ann Arbor: University of Michigan Press, 1963), pp. 75–76. Apparently in spy work these minor props are sometimes called an agent's "collection." Here see Monat, *op. cit.*, p. 163.

games are subject to constant development and change as new cues [30] are discovered, new instruments of observation perfected,[31] and once-secret techniques become familiar and thereby less effective.[32] (These developments, of course, are

[30] An interesting recent example is Eckhard Hess's work on pupil dilation as an indicator of attitude to an observed object. See E. Hess, "Attitude and Pupil Size," Scientific American, 212 (April 1965), 46–54; E. Hess and J. Polk, "Pupil Size as Related to Interest Value of Visual Stimuli," Science, 132, 3423 (August, 1960), 349–350.

[31] For example, in the history of smuggling, the invention of the cyclotron is a very recent event. The one at Witwatersrand University in South Africa can make diamonds radioactive, and some of these, replanted in diggings, allowed geiger counters to probe efficiently and relatively inoffensively for concealers and techniques of concealment. See J. du Plessis, Diamonds Are Forever (New York: John Day Co., 1964), pp. 86–87.

[32] For example, the use of "schedules" of radio transmission in order to convey strategic information from a hostile land to one's own country, the development of direction-finding equipment to pinpoint the place of transmission, and the development of speed tapes to reduce transmission time below what the finders require, or the use of spotters to follow after direction-finding vehicles and report in by telephone so that vulnerable transmissions in the vicinity can be postponed. See J. Whitwell, British Spy (London: William Kimber, 1966), p. 127. Or, in gambler-police games, the use of telephones to keep a business such as book-making private, the use of "taps" by the police to audit the calls, and then the use of decoy listed phones with distal extensions to defeat raids. Here see S. Dash, R. Knowlton, and R. Schwartz, The Eavesdroppers (New Brunswick: Rutgers University Press, 1959), pp. 237–238. Every criminal competence, in fact, seems to have its own expression game history. For example:

Narcotics are smuggled in numberless ways: in prunes where the pits ought to be; in hollowed millstones; under the habits of people distinguished as monks and nuns. More commonly, they are simply hidden in obscure corners of ships and planes and automobiles. And in the Middle East, the camel has often been the vehicle. Bedouins know all there is to know about camels, and one wizard among them discovered that he could stuff upwards of two dozen tins of narcotics down a camel's throat, and leave them there, clanking about in its stomach, for a month or more without undue protest from the camel. (Camels protest a great deal anyway.) Here, clearly, was a system with great potential. Thousands upon thousands of camels cross Middle Eastern borders every year. In time, of course, Customs officials got onto the scheme, but picking the right camels from among the thousands was something else again. Some tried poking the camels in the belly and listening for a tell-tale clink. But this was tiresome for the camel and risky for the investigator (camels are biters); besides, not everyone had the ear for it. Finally someone hit on the idea of mine detectors. These worked very well, until the Bedouins devised rubber containers for the narcotics. The camels, of course, must be slaughtered to get them out. [D. Lyle, "The Logistics of Junk," Esquire, March, 1966 (59–144), p. 61]

only one instance of the class, the other examples having to do with such matters as the evolution of safe-construction and safe-cracking techniques, submarine hiding and hunting devices, and the like.) Two particular developments in expression games are worth noting. First, as sophistication increases concerning what is given away through bodily expression, guardedness during face-to-face interaction may also increase; certainly it will shift in focus. Second, with the recent rapid advances in the technology of surveillance, there has been a marked extension in the kind of social setting that can be realistically suspected as insecure, that is, subject to monitoring; and with this we can expect an increase in care regarding certain expressions and an increase in willingness to be exposed regarding other expressions.

III   THE CONSTRAINTS ON PLAY

He who would analyze expression games must consider the ungamey conditions that gamesters must face whenever they engage in an actual game of expression. For the moves open to the subject are established by the restrictive conditions of play the observer faces, just as the ones open to the observer are established by the constraints affecting the subject. What one party must face as a limit on play the other party can exploit as a basis of advantage. Further, somewhat similar kinds of limitations face both subject and observer.

1.   The first constraint and condition to consider is derived from the interplay of three physical factors: what is to be hidden; what is to be used as cover; and the means of perception available to those from whom something is to be concealed. The interaction of these three basic elements generates both the possibilities of concealment and the currently inevitable limitations on concealing. Thus, during war, a factory can be camouflaged to look like a hospital from the air, but ground troops who approach close might not be possible to fool. The precise target and timing of a major invasion may

be concealable, but the required troops and supply are likely to be considered too massive to hide from anyone concerned,[33] and the planning so complex and so locked into sequence that once the action has begun, postponement becomes impractical.[34] A gym horse can effectively conceal the beginning of an escape tunnel and has, but if a whole company of armed men needs to be hidden, then something as large as the Trojan's horse will have to be employed. A man can conceal a vial of drugs by means of a suppository, but it will take a camel to conceal a whole box of it. Had the British S.O.E. been able to use large-denomination American bills to conduct its secret European work during World War II, sums up to a million dollars could have been quietly flown to London in one bag. However, since the money was needed in five- and ten-dollar bills, very bulky shipments had to be tactfully managed.[35] A bank robber could easily conceal on his person a loot of 20 or 30 high-denomination bills, but if he is foolish enough to scoop up ten rolls of pennies and two rolls of nickels, the pockets of his slacks may well give him away as he tries to appear "normal" on his way down the street.[36] Note, as previously suggested, technological developments constantly shift the relations among the covered, the cover, and uncovering perception: now that microphotography has been perfected, the front of a stamp can conceal a pageful of writing.

2. A general limitation on play is the state of the participants' technical knowledge and competence.

If the subject does not know about the kinds of cues in his own situation a sophisticated observer can use as a source of

---

[33] For example, the presence of friendly diplomatic corps free to move around and speak to strangers alone ensures that reports will be carried abroad to persons who happen to be in the pay of the enemy. See E. Montagu, *The Man Who Never Was* (New York: Bantam Books, 1964), p. 6.

[34] See, for example, Perrault, *op. cit.*, p. 154.

[35] Cookridge, *op. cit.*, p. 44.

[36] The sad story is reported in the *San Francisco Chronicle,* Sept. 29, 1965, under the lead, "Bulging Pockets Spoil Getaway."

information, then the subject can hardly obfuscate them (or accentuate them), were he desirous of doing so. Here we have, of course, one of the basic assumptions of projective tests such as the Rorschach, the doctrine being that since individuals censor their self-expressions one must rely on expressions they are not aware of giving off. Here, as already suggested in connection with culture-pattern slips, is to be seen one of the special problems of intelligence agents and others who attempt to pass as a native of a culture not their own. Natives never appreciate how well trained they are in the arts of detection until they find an alien among themselves who is trying to pass. Then ways of doing things that had always been taken for granted stand out by virtue of the presence of someone who is inadvertently doing the same things differently, as when milk is put in a cup before the tea, or the numeral four written with a crossing bar,[37] or pie eaten from the apex, not the side.

The observer faces similar limitations on his gaming. Clinically experienced physicians, for example, often can correctly distinguish soldiers who really have a disease from those who are faking symptoms; nonmedical observers are likely to be less skillful at this sorting procedure. Nor is sorting the real from the fake the only point at which technical knowledge is necessary. After gaining access to the real thing, an observer is of little use if he is not competent to learn something from what he is looking at. Modern advanced technology has thus brought great difficulties for our intelligence agencies:

> . . . the kind of man who is equipped by his training to breach [obstacles of access] is not likely to have the technical knowledge that will enable him to make a useful report on the complex targets that exist nowadays. If you don't know anything about nuclear reactors, there is little you can discover about one, even when you are standing right next to it.[38]

---

[37] Seth, *op. cit.*, pp. 153–156.
[38] Allen Dulles, *The Craft of Intelligence* (New York: Signet Books, 1965), p. 59.

3. A third set of constraints on the assessment game derives from what we can view commonsensically as the constitutive features of human players—their all-too-human nature, especially as subjects.

One such limitation is that of *emotional self-control.* When stakes are high or the inclination to escape is great, the subject needs much emotional self-control if he is not to give away through signs of uneasiness the fact that he may be guilty of what he is accused or suspected of. A guilty look, a furtive glance, an embarrassed hesitation, do not so much give the facts away as they do the fact that he knows the facts. In Eckman's term, what we have here are "deception clues" not "leakage." [39] In truth, even when the individual knows he is under scrutiny and knows what it is about his situation that the observer is scrutinizing, he may find that some sources of this expression are beyond his management. Thus no matter what a patient attempts to convey to his dentist concerning fearlessness, the dentist can estimate his patient's fear by the character of salivation—a symptom the patient is not likely to be able to bring under voluntary control, even should he learn that he is giving himself away by it. Similarly, although a student pilot may succeed in making a near perfect landing, his instructor will be able to tell, from the amount of body heat generated, the degree to which the neophyte is under pressure. The physiological indicators employed in the polygraph provide another example.[40]

---

[39] P. Eckman and W. Friesen, "Nonverbal Leakage and Clues to Deception," *Psychiatry,* 32 (1969), 88–106. "Deception clues tip him off that deception is in progress but do not reveal the concealed information; the betrayal of that withheld information we call leakage" (p. 89). Note that when the information sought by the observer is whether or not the subject is engaging in deception, then deception clues are leakage.

[40] We all function as lie detectors, of course, but our readings are presumably not as sensitive and reliable as true polygraphs, and cannot be trusted to be better at uncovering than our subject is at concealing, unless, as a student of panics suggests, conditions become very stressful:

Under any circumstances, however, when the fear of an individual attains a certain intensity, it becomes impossible to prevent all overt manifestation of the emotion. A check may be kept on such very gross behavior as

Here, it should be noted, the study of expression games has close bearing on the study of face-to-face gatherings. The propriety of an individual's activity is largely determined by the allocation of his involvement: he is obliged to maintain involvement in suitable matters and disattend unsuitable ones.[41] Natural units of face-to-face interaction are built up from these involvements. A conversational encounter, for example, is owed the involvement of its ratified participants, just as the neighboring conversations have a claim on civil disattendance. Constant monitoring occurs, whereby everyone checks up on the stability of the situation by noting the propriety of the persons in it, this itself accomplished by checking up on the allocation of involvement manifest by everyone present. The perceivable direction of an individual's gaze provides perhaps the chief source of information concerning his involvements. Given these circumstances, it is understandable that an individual who feels he is improperly involved will try to conceal the direction of his gaze and otherwise mask his involvement. (Thus, when a subject turns to find that an observer appears to have been looking at him, the subject

---

screaming, or uncoordinated gesturing, but the same cannot be done for such bodily reactions as trembling, paling, sweating, high-pitchedness of voice, dilation of eye pupils, etc. There are expressions of the emotion which involuntarily appear when fear attains a certain degree of intensity. In fact, the individual may often not even be aware at the moment that he is exhibiting the physical manifestations of fear. For example, a physician who fled in panic during an earthquake noted that the voices of the people he came in contact with were pitched high, which helped to sustain his own fear. This eventually led him to wonder and finally to realize that he too was talking shrilly.

Whether or not an individual is aware of expressing such involuntary signs of fear, the important fact is that any or all of them serve, if detected by others within an appropriate context, as a form of unintentional communication. If an individual is afraid enough, he will quite unwittingly and often unconsciously manifest certain physical reactions which other people, given relevant circumstances, will interpret as indicating a felt fear on his part. [E. Quarantelli, "A Study of Panic: Its Nature, Types and Conditions," Master's Thesis, University of Chicago, Department of Sociology, 1953, p. 144]

[41] Developed in E. Goffman, *Behavior in Public Places* (New York: The Free Press, 1963).

may continue his gaze forward as if merely scanning the room so as not to betray an interest in someone he has no good reason to be interested in. Similarly, when a girl kisses a boy she may elect to keep her eyes closed so that should he open his he will be unable to see that she is involved in something other than the business at hand, and further, be unable to see that she has seen that he has seen this.) Now the point is that a subject can rarely be in complete self-control of these expressions. When a subject attempts to conceal his wariness of something at hand, it is nearly certain that he will give himself away through expressions perceived by himself and others as signs of self-consciousness and ill-ease. And the more he is concerned to mask his actual involvement, the more self-conscious he may appear. Here we have, then, a significant matter in the social organization of persons present to one another, and significant also in considering the natural incapacities of gamesmen who must play their game under the immediate gaze of opponents. Incidentally, it is this incapacity to inhibit warning signs of self-consciousness that makes an individual relatively safe to be near.

I have suggested that subjects cannot be counted on to maintain complete strategic control over their expressive behavior. A related human weakness pertains to the sustaining of intellectual control. If a subject can be questioned at length, and if he responds with many statements, he may find it intellectually difficult not to give himself away through inconsistencies and inadvertent slips. Astute reporters play this game against government officials.[42]

The strategic significance of a subject's limit regarding emotional and intellectual control is nicely illustrated in the well-developed arts of police interrogation.[43] The interrogator assumes that the subject either does not know that he knows

---

[42] See for example, Dulles, *op. cit.*, 224. When the subject is a team of persons, of course, consistency with respect to what is admitted is even more precarious.

[43] I am grateful here to an unpublished paper (1962) by Sally Davis.

important facts, or knows that he knows them and is trying to conceal them. The interrogator then sets about to press the subject's capacity as a gamesman to the breaking point. To this end, the interrogator may take such actions and make such allegations as are calculated to cause his victim to become and remain "nervous" and "out of control" of himself and the situation, unable thus to mobilize himself fully for the game of expression.[44] In police interrogation, the subject may be kept waiting; [45] told that smoking is not allowed;[46] bodily prevented from doodling, from shifting in his chair or from otherwise finding a nervous release;[47] accorded an off-putting term of address; [48] responded to with overlong silences,[49] or a close direct look in the eyes.[50] Of course, if the subject can be made to feel that he is playing the game of covering badly, then this very realization can reduce his self-control and his capacity to cover:

---

[44] In ordinary sociable interaction, participants often manifest the opposite concern; they limit themselves to those actions which will not make others present feel ill at ease, and when others are ill at ease, may take as their first obligation the reduction of this tension. Occupational as well as social reasons are to be found for such engineering. Thus, photographers may seek out devices for putting their subjects at ease:

We must remember that a portrait sitting is an extremely artificial situation. The poor sitter feels constantly observed, put to a test, not only by the critical eye of the *photographer* but also by the pitiless lens of the camera. He feels awkward, self-conscious, intimidated, and absolutely unnatural. Very few people are able to lose their self-consciousness immediately and behave in front of the camera as though it were not there. In most cases the photographer has to help the subject. [P. Halsman, "Psychological Portraiture," *Popular Photography*, December 1958, p. 121]

It should be recognized that the techniques for making another ill at ease or comfortable belong to the very general game of manipulating the other's capacity for controlled behavior, as when a gamesman says something to throw his opponent off his stroke or make him box imprudently. Loss of self-control in an expression game is merely one consequence of loss of composure.

[45] R. Arthur and R. Caputo, *Interrogation for Investigators* (New York: William C. Copp, 1959), p. 31.

[46] *Ibid.*, pp. 26–28.

[47] *Ibid.*, chapter X, "The Nervous Suspect," pp. 91–111.

[48] *Ibid.*, pp. 33–34.

[49] *Ibid.*, pp. 33–34.

[50] *Ibid.*, p. 75.

An offender who is led to believe that his appearance and demeanor are betraying him is thereby placed in a much more vulnerable position. His belief that he is exhibiting symptoms of guilt has the effect of destroying or diminishing his confidence in his ability to deceive and tends to convince him of the futility of further resistance. This attitude, of course, places him much nearer the confession stage.[51]

Although an accelerated pulsation of the carotid artery in the neck is experienced by some innocent persons as well as a certain number of guilty ones, such a phenomenon exhibited by a guilty subject can be commented upon to good advantage.[52]

For much the same reason, and in much the same way as with No. 1 above, it is well to comment upon the over-activity of a subject's epiglottis or Adam's apple.[53]

When a subject fails to look the interrogator straight in the eye (and looks at the floor, wall, or ceiling instead), or when he exhibits a restlessness by leg-swinging, foot-wiggling, hand-wringing, finger-tapping, the picking of his fingernails, or the fumbling with objects such as a tie clasp or pencil, it is well for the interrogator to get the idea across that he is aware of such reactions and that he views them as manifestations of lying.[54]

What we have here is a direct assault on the frame of conventional spoken interaction, namely an intentional shifting into the explicit focus of attention of what is ordinarily obligatorily disattended.[55]

The human nature of the subject brings a further limitation to his gamesmanship. When engaging in a control move he will be consciously aware of the discrepancy between appearances and the facts. To retain control, as suggested,

---

[51] F. Inbau and J. Reid, *Criminal Interrogation and Confessions* (Baltimore: Williams and Wilkins, 1962), p. 29.

[52] *Ibid.*, p. 30.

[53] *Ibid.*, p. 30.

[54] *Ibid.*, p. 30.

[55] A further analysis of the process is attempted in E. Goffman, "Fun in Games," in *Encounters* (Indianapolis: Bobbs Merrill, 1961), pp. 52–53.

he will here have to suppress effectively those many signs through which he can give himself away; he will have to act cooly and unsuspiciously even when the observer is getting warm and close to discovery. But, of course, something more is involved.

Knowing the discrepancy between the facts and appearances, the subject will have command of the words to convey the real facts. This is a special contingency of human agents. Although a room can be searched for missing gems, its arm cannot be twisted to disclose the hiding place. A dog can give his master's hiding place away expressively by looks and movements, and he may even intentionally lead rescuers to the place where his master lies injured; but he cannot be induced to squeal. Persons can be—unless they can avoid the persuasion by successfully feigning death, insanity, or ignorance.

When, then, an individual hides such things as contraband or strategic plans, he must not only be skilled at the material task of concealment and (what is quite a different property) possess sufficient emotional self-control and intellectual control so as not to give away strategic information inadvertently; but in addition he must refrain from willfully communicating his secret. As suggested, when human gamesters are found out, they can save the day by offering convincing accountings; but the same ability makes them able to communicate the facts before the facts are otherwise discovered.

We can say that anyone who hides something away and then keeps his lips sealed, or reveals something through communication that he had theretofore hidden, does so because he feels his interests can be furthered in this way. Now "interests" have a special status. First, individuals can and are likely to share them, thereby becoming a team playing an expression game against another team. Second, except perhaps in recreational games, it can never be said that an individual has only one interest. Individuals aren't like that. Ordinarily, of course, the individual will be officially active in connection with one set of interests, and there will be some understanding and agreement that his other interests are temporarily set aside although unscheduled appearance itself can be officially allowed for under certain circumstances. A jurisdiction of place, time, and importance will prevail. Events may occur, however, and moreover can be made to occur, which cause his latent other interests suddenly to become very manifest. Then a conflict that was always potential becomes manifest. And this, of course, is how uncovering through pressure occurs.[56] By acutely awakening the subject's ordinarily latent interests he, in effect, becomes split in two, with one of these interest-serving persons forming a coalition with the enemy.[57] There are standard methods of mobilizing these interests.

There is *seduction* in its various forms. The observer's object here is to maneuver a definition of the situation such that the subject is led to believe that the observer is to be treated as something of a teammate, to whom strategic information (among other things) can be voluntarily entrusted. To this end the observer may invoke such moral and religious norms as are calculated to cause the subject to feel that he and the observer support the same general interests—a technique that seems too simple for self-respecting gamesters to use, and yet is widely used effectively in everyday life.[58] In addition to seduction through ideological appeal, there is the social kind: the observer can cultivate the kind of social relationship to his subject such that candor and trust on the latter's part becomes a natural expression of the bond. For example, police interrogators systematically employ moral

---

[56] This is how compliance of all kinds can be obtained, but here we are interested in only one type of compliance, albeit an important one, namely, the giving up of information.

[57] In intelligence work the enemy can be "within," as when an agent devotes too much of his time to the care and profit of his cover occupation, or transmits fictional information just to appear worth his pay.

[58] Even in the exigencies of police work this technique seems to be relied on. See, for example, Inbau and Reid, *op. cit.*, pp. 56–57, and Arthur and Caputo, *op. cit.*, p. 138.

sympathy as a means of inducing confessions from suspects.[59] Moreover, police instructors specifically encourage their students to treat stool pigeons "decently," that is, as persons worthy of personal relationships (in spite of the popular contempt felt for them), presumably because this policy pays:

> The ability of the individual officer or a law enforcement organization to obtain and hold informers depends, we think, on many considerations, perhaps the first of which is a reputation for integrity and fair dealing. It is sometimes easy for the policeman, who is a one-shot operator, to obtain an informer on representation and glib promises which are not carried out. But a department tolerating this practice too will find it is cut off from much worthwhile information. Fairness is one of the most admired of human virtues. The officer who hopes to continue in the useful employment of informers must never misrepresent to them in matters affecting the informer personally.[60]

It might be added that before this social seduction can occur it may be necessary for the seducer to assume a false identity, as when a detective in disguise begins a bar friendship with someone whom he is keeping under surveillance—what in criminal and police circles is sometimes called "roping." [61]

Seduction as a means by which the observer can attempt to break the subject's cover is to be distinguished, I feel, from *coercive exchange*, that is, the kind of exchange which the subject participates in under pressure and in spite of his finer feelings in the matter.[62] Here the observer frankly tries to

---

[59] H. Mulbar, *Interrogation* (Springfield: Charles Thomas, 1951), pp. 6, 10; Arthur and Caputo, *op. cit.*, pp. 35–36, 64–65, 108–109.

[60] M. Harney and J. Cross, *The Informer in Law Enforcement* (Springfield: Charles Thomas, 1962), p. 52.

[61] Jacob Fisher, *The Art of Detection* (Sterling Paperbacks, 1961), p. 108.

[62] There is a distinct tendency in the social sciences to analyze seduction as merely one type of exchange, defining such things as deference and regard as goods that can be traded in for whatever other commodities that can be gotten for them. I feel that this is a very questionable procedure. During the course of ordinary everyday dealings between individuals, psychic indulgences may flow from one to another, but as a running comment on the state of the relationship not as something that has been openly bargained for. The net results of the dealings can be some sort of balance of indulgences on both

arrange to involve the subject in a *quid pro quo* such that the subject, with no necessary diminution of antagonism to the observer, may yet find it in his private interests to divulge what he could otherwise conceal, or conceal what he would otherwise reveal. Bribery can be involved, where the subject is offered something he desires in exchange for voluntary divulgence or concealment that betrays what he had been loyal to, the resulting deal being one that is repugnant to him. (The list of bribes is long. Thus police informants are said to sing in order to cop a plea, to obtain revenge, to eliminate competitors, to obtain money, and to obtain information about their own situation.[63]) Blackmail can be involved, where the subject accedes to the other's wishes in exchange for the latter's silence in a matter that would destroy the subject's reputation, were it known—a matter that the observer may have engineered the subject into creating in the first place.[64] Physical threat may be involved, where the subject is offered release from pain or from imprisonment or from a death sentence in exchange for information, or in exchange for any other act that can be performed at the moment in the immediate presence of the threat.[65]

---

sides, especially when the participants are status equals, but this balance is a consequence of a properly affirmed relationship, not an aim or end of action. And should an observer indulge his subject with malice aforethought, merely to obtain an indulgence in return, he will still have to style his behavior as though he had other interests, else he will not, in general, be successful in his aims. On types of exchange, see E. Goffman, *Asylums* (Garden City: Doubleday Anchor, 1961), pp. 275–278. An interesting treatment of these general issues is presented in K. Boulding, "Towards a Pure Theory of Threat Systems," *Defense and Disarmament*, American Economic Association, pp. 424–434. Robert Jervis has suggested that there are situations in which something can be gained by making it evident that one's apparent expressions are calculated.

[63] Harney and Cross, *op. cit.*

[64] In the intelligence game, engineered blackmail is often employed in conjunction with payments in a kind of combined appeal, as illustrated, for example, in the Russian handling of Vassall during World War II. In fiction, those who employ coercive exchange are usually less shrewd and limit themselves to this one device.

[65] Personal threat cannot be used to induce a subject to perform an act that requires his unaccompanied movement in the free community unless the coercer has a pervasive network of fellow agents, a strategic capacity imputed to the Cosa Nostra, the NKVD, and SMERSH. The value to the observer of

Corresponding to these "natural" weaknesses in the subject and his game, there are some to be found in the observer and his game. As will be considered later, the observer is likely to try to conceal from the subject the strategic fact that assessment is occurring. The observer himself thus becomes vulnerable; he, like the subject, becomes vulnerable to self-exposure through various failures of self-control. Further, when the observer is but one of the members of a team, then his human nature renders him vulnerable to seduction and coercion in the manner already discussed. The only difference is that a subject under pressure may inform the other side, whereas an observer under pressure may fail to inform his own side— much the same kind of lapse albeit one that is easier to conceal. Interestingly, this failure to inform may be produced not by the enemy but by one's own team, this being the age-old problem of communicating to a tyrant. Thus, it is said that Hitler reduced the information he received from Gehlen about the Russian reserves, and the information he received from Schellenberg about American war potential, by acting as if bad news was the fault of the informant.[66]

Both subject and observer, then, have natural weaknesses which mar their game and give advantage to the other side. But matters are more complicated still. The frailty of subjects under torture does cause them to reveal secrets, but the same frailty will lead them to say anything to bring an end to the persuasion, and this, the interrogator can appreciate, renders doubtful all admissions obtained in this way:

---

obtaining a hostage lies not merely in the possibility that the subject will have greater feelings for it than for himself, but that immediate physical threat to the hostage can be maintained by one or two captors while the subject is forced to do things against his will in a place he himself is perfectly safe in. Note that torture seems to have a marginal status, analytically speaking, apart from the fact that it is not morally nice. Information imparted while crazed with pain can be considered a kind of involuntary uncontrollable expression; information imparted after the torture has been halted by an involuntary cry of submission might be considered differently, namely, as participation in a coercive exchange.

[66] Perrault, op. cit., pp. 170–171.

Apart from its inherent loathsomeness and the fact, for which we may devoutly thank God, that evidence extracted under duress is not admissible in a British court of law, physical torture has one overwhelming disadvantage. Under its spur an innocent man will often confess to some crime he has never committed, merely to gain a respite. If he has been badly tortured, he will even invent a crime involving the death penalty, preferring quick death to a continuation of his agony. Physical torture will ultimately make any man talk but it cannot ensure that he will tell the truth.[67]

During the Inquisition in Europe, persons suspected of witchcraft often knew precisely what they must confess in order to allow the interrogator to feel he could stop his inquiry; and knowing what to say, said it. It was in the eighteenth century that judges finally decided that the confessions extracted from the accused by torture ought really not be trusted or acted upon.[68]

Thus, the weakness of the subject can become a drawback for the observer. More important, the subject can come to strategic terms with his own weaknesses and even exploit them to improve his game. He can assess his own limitations and act accordingly, as when a person who knows he cannot bluff convincingly elects, for this reason, not to attempt to do so. Here the subject splits himself in two, as it were, with one of his selves taking action relative to the proclivities of the other. A more pronounced version of the same splitting can be found in situations where the individual, at a point in time, binds his own hands in regard to a later time—a time when his will and capacity might be weak or his desires different. He thus renders himself a more reliable instrument than he is, as when, not trusting himself, he places the alarm clock out of easy reach the night before when his resolve is strong and he is in full charge of himself, or he establishes a

---

[67] Pinto, *op. cit.*, p. 25.
[68] H. Trevor-Roper, "Witches and Witchcraft," *Encounter*, 28, 5 (May 1967), 3–25; 28, 6 (June 1967), 13–34.

weekly credit maximum in a casino long before the occasion arises when he would overextend himself. The famous poison pill of the intelligence agent is another case in point, as every schoolboy, these days, knows. A similar split use of the self occurs when a bank robber, seeing that he is seen to be shaking, warns the teller, "I'm very nervous. Be careful or I'll shoot."

When the subject is a team instead of a person, of course splitting as a device to improve play is naturally facilitated. A conventional example is found in selective recruitment, as when intelligence agents are selected in advance as persons whose pasts and presents offer fewest bases for mobilizing divergent interest. Just as common is the practice of obliging the individual to act for his team without knowing the personal identity of the other members (as when agents transmit documents through a "cut out" or a "dead drop"), or without knowing the overall plan of his side—an ignorance that has allowed ambassadors to be genuine in their protestations of friendship even when their own countries were about to invade. Obviously, ignorance renders individuals incapable of betraying their proper interests, although no one has devised a means of convincing the opponent of this ignorance, and therefore saving captured agents painful ordeals.

Behind this use of ignorance as a means of protecting the team, there is, of course, an understanding about the limitations of human subjects as gamesmen. A person is a thing of which too much can be asked, and if everything must be asked, it will be at the asker's peril. A ship can be scuttled and a bomb sight shattered in order to avoid their falling into enemy hands; but, apparently, in spite of romantic literature, it is not wise for an intelligence agency to rely on its agents committing suicide when the proper time comes.[69]

---

[69] Felix, *op. cit.*, pp. 100–101. In discussing the role in strategic interaction of the destruction button the Russians claim to have found in Powers' U-2 plane, Felix asks whether it is better for an intelligence agency to cover its action by having a pilot scuttle his plane, scuttle himself and his plane, or be scuttled, unbeknownst to himself, along with his plane.

The point here, however, is that a team cannot only allow for this very human weakness but also can actively exploit it. It has been suggested by some students of intelligence practices that the British, during the last war, desiring to mislead the Germans regarding the time and place of the anticipated invasion, employed the following device: they gave London-trained resistance workers false confidential invasion information and suicide pills that were placebos, and then parachuted them into the hands of agents suspected of being "turned," or gave them transmission channels calculated to be intercepted —all this to ensure that captures would be made and that, under torture, someone would probably break and provide his interrogators with a perfect performance.[70] This is an extreme example. The principle is also employed in less tortuous circumstances, but with the same purpose of getting an individual to act naturally in a role because, in fact, he does not know that he is playing a false one. For example, take the design of the "Man Who Never Was" operation during World War II—wherein a high-level courier carrying secret papers containing misdirections regarding the Mediterranean invasion was to be washed up on the coast of Spain. After the "Major" was dropped in Spanish waters, the British attaché in Spain was "confidentially" told that papers of great importance had been lost, and that he should discreetly determine whether the courier's briefcase had been recovered. The attaché was thus able to act out his part in the fake-out in a very convincing manner by virtue of the fact that for him it wasn't an act.[71]

4. I have mentioned three types of limitation on the play of expression games: physical factors, knowledge, and "human nature." A final constraint to consider is that of social norms.

Take the subject first. Although varying from one social circle to another, and from one set of circumstances to another, there is nonetheless a special morality about impression

---

[70] See Perrault, *op. cit.*, ch. 24, "Deceit and Sacrifice."
[71] Ind, *op. cit.*, pp. 176–177.

management. There are rules against communicating self-disbelieved statements. There are even rules about merely inhibiting one's expression and communication. Thus, American intelligence, in the last war, is credited with having recruited as a spy a French monk, who was shortly caught when a German officer routinely asked him where he was going, the monk having then felt obliged to say that he was spying, lest he tell a lie.[72] The nineteenth century provides an even more touching illustration: apparently the gentlemanly code was such that European officers disdained to lead camouflaged men on camouflaged missions, demanding that their soldiers wear dazzling and readily visible uniforms and do battle at openly agreed-upon times and places—else a desire for unsportsman and unmanly advantage might be imputed.[73] Most important, there are expectations of a normative kind regarding "sincerity." We demand that when an individual speaks, his bodily expression will provide easy access to all the information needed in order to determine how much self-belief and resolve lies behind his statements. Differently put, we demand of an individual that he not be too good at acting, especially during occasions of talk.[74]

Parenthetically, it might be noted here that limitations on the subject's play that are due to lack of emotional self-control and limitations that are due to norms and moral rules have an important bearing on each other. Once norms are incorporated, their infraction is likely to lead the actor to display

---

[72] Alsop and Braden, *op. cit.*, p. 37.

[73] It is thus that Eric Ambler accounts for the absence of spy stories before the twentieth century. Only in modern times did such a fellow come to be thought of as potentially heroic material. See E. Ambler, ed., *To Catch a Spy* (New York: Athenaeum, 1965), pp. 12–13.

[74] Sincerity has some additional, even paradoxical meanings. We may say of a person that he is sincere when he provides us with an expansive emotional display when making an avowal. And we say of a stage actor that he is sincere when he gives the appearance of being "natural," that is, of not acting, at a time when he is indeed officially engaged in acting. Derivations of this latter use allow colleagues to praise a fellow-salesman for his sincerity, when, in fact, what is meant is that he can effectively mislead customers by enacting expressive assurances.

uncontrollable minor signs of guilt, shame, and embarrass-
ment, and he will display these signs long after he has ceased
to be bound by the norm in crucial situations. Thus, many
persons are willing to try to tell a bald lie, but few persons
can manage to do so without expressing in some way that
they are not telling the truth. And, of course, these giveaway
signs can be strategically crucial when opponents are in one
another's immediate presence. (Norms, then, serve as an indirect as well as direct limitation on moves in expression
games, especially covering moves.)

I have suggested that subjects are constrained by morality.
Observers are held in check by norms, too.

For example, spying tends to be considered repugnant,
always by the party spied upon, sometimes by those who
employ spies, and occasionally even by spies themselves.
Moreover, there are legal penalties attached to many forms
of spying.

Similar contingencies are associated with the conduct of
examinations. In many informal social circles it is felt to be
improper for one individual to doubt another's expressions or
statements, or to probe intrusively into what might be called
his informational territory. Those who conduct criminal examinations are also restrained, this time by law more than by
custom. If a subject's confession is to hold up in an American
court, he must be warned ahead of time that anything he says
will be held against him.[75] All kinds of chicanery can be employed by the observer to make the subject feel that there is
firm evidence against him and that it is useless to dissemble
further, but devices must not be used against the guilty which
would make an innocent person confess; [76] in fact, the interrogator may lose his own status as a witness should he employ
these methods with the subject.[77] Thus, prolonged interrogation can invalidate the avowals obtained in this way, although,

---

[75] Inbau and Reid, *op. cit.*, pp. 162ff., and Mulbar, *op. cit.*, pp. 62ff.

[76] Inbau and Reid, *op. cit.*, pp. 140ff.

[77] *Ibid.*, pp. 187–188.

incidentally, if other facts can be uncovered by using this ill-got information, these other facts can be used as evidence.[78] Confessions obtained by threats against liberty, limbs, or loved ones are also invalid. Promises to reduce or eliminate legal penalties can be defined as out of bounds, although promises of greater comfort are not.[79] Lie detector tests may not be admissible unless the subject and the observer attestably agree to admissibility beforehand. And information acquired by examining the contents from a forcibly pumped stomach,[80] or by obtaining statement while the subject is under the influence of the so-called truth drugs,[81] may not only not be used in court, but acquisition of knowledge in this way may itself be subject to court penalty. In the courts themselves there are, of course, constitutional restrictions on forcing a subject to testify on a matter that is likely to incriminate him. Also various statutes may relieve him from having to divulge the secrets of his spouse or patient or legal client or parishioner.

It is also the case that seduction is everywhere considered with some disapproval. Coercive exchange is even more disapproved. In most contexts it is not only morally repugnant but also illegal for an interrogator to establish the circumstances in which he can offer to cease torturing a subject in exchange for information.

A final comment about the norms that constrain subjects and observers. These various rules of play can be followed, and gamesmanship correspondingly constrained, for a variety of reasons, good and bad: incorporation of the norms, causing an offender to feel guilt when he deviates even secretly; genuine concern for the good opinion of witnesses, causing feelings of shame when this is threatened; fear of legal penalty; perceived long-range expedience, and so forth.

---

[78] *Ibid.*, pp. 190–191.
[79] *Ibid.*, pp. 183–184.
[80] *Ibid.*, p. 191.
[81] *Ibid.*, pp. 189–190.

IV THE STRATEGIC PROPERTIES OF PLAY

Just as certain properties of players have a special significance in expression games, so do certain properties of play
itself.

1.   Note should be taken, first, of the difference between *real*
moves and *virtual* or *tacit* ones. As G. H. Mead argued, when
an individual considers taking a course of action, he is likely
to hold off until he has imagined in his mind the consequence
of his action for others involved, their likely response to this
consequence, and the bearing of this response on his own
designs. He then modifies his action so that it now incorporates that which he calculates will usefully modify the other's
generated response. In effect, he adapts to the other's response before it has been called forth, and adapts in such a
way that it never does have to be made. He has thus incorporated tacit moves into his line of behavior. Now when the
courses of action, actual and imagined, consist of assessment
and response to assessment we find ourselves dealing with
virtual or tacit moves in an expression game. The observer
imagines the likely consequence of the subject discovering
that he is being assessed, and attempts to offset the likely
control of impression before it has had a chance to occur. Thus
the observer's first and second moves, constituting moves
of the naïve and uncovering types, are collapsed into one.

For example, a standard surveillance procedure is wire tapping. However, if the subject whose wire is being tapped
knows that tapping is occurring, then the tap is of little use.
The observer knows this and knows that the subject is likely
to become suspicious of a tap should he hear the clicking
sounds characteristic of a tap being cut in. To counter this
giveaway, the observer can use a variable resistor so that the
connection is only gradually effected and no noise occurs.[82]

---

[82] Dash, Knowlton, and Schwartz, *op. cit.*, p. 317.

Only one concrete act results—a special way of cutting into a telephone line—but it contains moves of two types in the expression game.

Another example is found in the game of surveillance where the observer's purpose is to keep the subject within observation without his learning that he is being observed, and the subject's concern is to know when he is under observation and, if possible, to rid himself of observers. When the subject rides off in a car, vehicular tailing is likely to be employed. Here are the complications: The observer assumes that if the subject discovers that he is being tailed he will take evasive action in order to shake or lose the tail and that he will put off engaging in incriminating, that is, informationally vital acts. If the subject succeeds in this, he wins the contest. To avoid losing the contest, the observer will adjust his distance from the subject's car so that it can be kept in view but not from so close a distance as to render the subject suspicious, the assumption being that he may be anxious enough and wily enough to keep checking through his rear-view mirror. Where travel time is long or traffic is either very heavy or thin, the maintenance of this safe distance will be very difficult. On such occasions the observer may find it advisable to use multiple tailing units in two-way radio contact. After a block or two, and well before suspicion is likely to be aroused, one tail can turn off and radio a second to pick up the trail at the next intersection. When extra cars cannot be brought into play, the observer himself can try to provide the subject with the kind of evidence he is likely to accept as demonstrating that the car that might have appeared to be tailing him really is not: the observer can pass the subject a couple of times, each time, of course, allowing himself to be overtaken and repassed by his quarry. However, the subject may appreciate that someone tailing him may employ just this passing dodge as a means of avoiding suspicion. In any case, the observer may well feel that the subject may have this feeling. It behooves the observer, then, to provide a countering move to suspicion that his initial countering action may have produced. Darkness will help:

> At night it is easier for one car to maintain a tail. The investigator conducting this type of night activity should occasionally pass the subject of the investigation on a clear road. Some investigators have a special switch installed on their dashboards permitting the extinguishing of either one or both of the tail lights without affecting the headlights. By this subterfuge, it will appear that a car with one tail light passed the suspect the first time, a car with two tail lights the second time, and a car with no tail lights at the third passing. It is possible also to install lenses in the tail light with dashboard control which may show the lights red or colorless. The investigator should remember when driving without lights or when the tail lights are switched off that his foot brake will cause a light to flash when applied. Proper adjustment in advance will rectify this giveaway.[83]

Now obviously, the observer can engage in all of these tricks without the subject suspecting any car; and certainly it is common for the observer to use these devices even though he never acquires firm evidence that the subject at any time thought he was being followed. The tacit interplay of moves, then, may (but need not be) quite one-sided. A player can counter an action that has not, in fact, been taken. He acts on the basis of a tacit interplay of moves.

Just as the observer's response projects the subject's tacit move into the play, so does the subject's response project the observer's. Control moves and counter-uncovering moves are very often made before the move to which they are a response has had a chance to occur. For example, when an "illegal," is constructed, that is, when someone is given a personal or biographical identity not his own, his spurious social past must be "back-stopped"; *before* those among whom he is planted have a chance to check up on his stated background, the

---

[83] Fisher, *op. cit.*, p. 91.

places and records they might appeal to must be got to and the necessary arrangements made.[84] Another example may be cited. It is a general fact that when an observer does finally learn what a subject knows, the observer may still have to worry about the possibility that the subject may himself have been misinformed by his own team as part of routine cover, this being a general implication of the standard task of minimizing the number of people in the know. The subject may feel it wise to take this possibility into consideration, as illustrated in the "Man Who Never Was" operation:

> If the German General Staff was to be persuaded in face of all probabilities, to bank on our next target being somewhere other than Sicily, it would have to have before it a document which was passing between officers who must know what our real plans were, who could not possibly be mistaken and who could not themselves be the victims of a cover plan. If the operation was to be worthwhile, I had to have a document written by someone, and to someone, whom the Germans knew—and whom they knew to be "right in the know." [85]

It should now be apparent that not only can a player's move be a response to a tacit move on the other's part, but may have to be if it is to be effective. Precautions not taken before the opponent has had a chance to make his move may not be worth taking at all, and the player may clearly appreciate that this is the case. We must then expect the taking of some overprecautions, we must expect some insuring, some diffusion of wariness, some adaptation to moves which one knows the opponent may not even have considered making.
2. An important feature of expression games has to do with the significance for the play of the player's knowledge of the other's knowledge of what is occurring in the game. For the play itself has its own strategic implications.

---

[84] Dulles, *op. cit.*, p. 61. In police work, a rookie cop who is to be used as a plant may be let go from the Police Academy on grounds of possessing a criminal record which, in fact, has been documented for him. See Dash, Knowlton, and Schwartz, *op. cit.*, p. 254.

[85] Montagu, *op. cit.*, p. 23.

Here the term "secret" can be imprecise. The information the observer is trying to acquire is very often information the subject already has, being therefore no secret to him; the subject's concern is to restrict access to it. In addition, sometimes the subject is concerned to keep the observer from knowing that the subject has this information and is guarding it. This, of course, is another bit of guarded information, but this time information about information. It is this last that might be called a secret. Should the observer succeed in obtaining access to the subject's guarded information, the observer will almost always find it in his interests to conceal that he has done so, lest the subject act so as to neutralize the value to the observer of possessing it and destroy the possibility of his acquiring more information in the same manner. The observer makes a secret of his discovery, that is, he restricts access to information about his information. (But, of course, what he is secretly informed about is something that the subject knows; the subject does not know merely that the observer has discovered it.[86]) It is typical then that when restricted documents are intercepted by an intelligence agent, he photographs or memorizes them and tries to return them in such a manner that it will not be seen that they have been seen. We can thus understand why cryptographers are plagued with the dilemma of wanting to make use of decoded materials, yet not wanting through this to warn the enemy that his code has been broken, lest the code be changed and the breaking have to be done all over again.[87]

It is clear, then, that when one individual engages in assessing another, it will be in his interests to control information about this fact, information about having made either a naïve or an uncovering move in an expression game. The very act by which the observer checks up on the subject can jeopardize the observer's position, should the subject discover that this effort is occurring; for this discovery may put the subject

[86] Felix, *op. cit.*, pp. 114–115.
[87] B. Tuchman, *The Zimmerman Telegram* (New York: Delta Paperback), p. 10. See also Dulles, *op. cit.*, pp. 74–75.

on his guard, increase his care, alter his plans, cause him to see that the observer is prepared to engage in what is only a show of trust in others, and certainly disillusion the subject about his relationship to the observer. It follows, in turn, that the arousal of suspicion in another so that he suspects he is being suspected can be a strategic loss. Criminals who expose the fact that they are trying to find out what the police know or suspect can thereby give themselves away:

> When an innocent driver meets and passes a Traffic Patrol, it is improbable that either will slow down and watch the other through his driving mirror. So when, through mine, I noticed the driver of a sports car doing exactly this, I turned and went after him and, in due course, he and his pal did a month each for taking it.[88]

The importance of secrecy on the part of the observer is well appreciated in the arts of interrogation and forms an integral part of the interrogation game. This game can be played in a pure form when the subject takes the position that he has nothing to hide and is willing to be cooperative with his interrogator. Traditional moves are open to the latter. He is likely to find it useful to tell the subject as little as possible about what they both know but the subject does not know that the interrogator knows. The interrogator can then trap the subject into a lie that can be exposed, thus weakening the subject's maneuverability in regard to matters that the observer doesn't know about.[89] And whether the subject is led to tell a lie or leads himself to tell one, it will be advisable for the observer to refrain from confronting him immediately, but rather to await some more useful and delicate time to do so.[90] (Note, however, that there will be times when the interrogator will be advised to refrain from putting a question to which a lying answer is likely, since once the

[88] V. Meek, *Cops and Robbers* (London: Duckworth, 1962), p. 105.

[89] Inbau and Reid, *op. cit.*, p. 98.

[90] Arthur and Caputo, *op. cit.*, pp. 51–52.

subject is committed to a lie, he will exhibit increased defensiveness, having something further to conceal.) [91] Another traditional move is for the interrogator to ask questions of the subject which imply, but falsely, that the interrogator already has part of the information—the possibility being, of course, that the subject will unwarily confirm what is only suspected.[92]

It follows that once a subject has established a relationship to the observer that obliges the subject to attend to the other's questions, then questions will likely be available to which any answer—including no answer—weakens the subject's strategic position. For example, a man suspected of being an agent, protesting that he is not, and asked when he last saw a named person likely to be his contact, has to decide whether to display unfamiliarity with the name, familiarity but remote association, or the actual truth concerning the last meet; and most important, he must choose his move without appearing to think first, for if he hesitates he provides a "deception clue," and discredits his claimed relationship to the interrogator.[93]

Just as the observer must be concerned about the implications of his playing an expression game, so the subject must be concerned about the implications of *his* own playing. For the subject is likely to find that he cannot attempt to cover his tracks without exposing himself to some risk that his efforts will be discovered as such. Should this discovery occur it can have short-run consequences for him apart from the question of his reputation and self-image; and these consequences of discovery must be weighted by the probability of their occurring and balanced off against the gains possible from concealment. The consequences are as follows: when the observer catches the subject out trying to control impres-

---

[91] *Ibid.*, p. 42.

[92] Inbau and Reid, *op. cit.*, p. 99.

[93] See for example, A. W. Sansom, *I Spied Spies* (London: Harrap, 1965), p. 36.

sions, the observer acquires advantageous information, for in knowing that all is not as it seems and that a conscious effort has been made to rig appearances, he will often be able to narrow down considerably the range of things that might actually be going on. For example, if the subject is a police-suspect, the discovery that he has falsified evidence exposes him as someone who has quite probably committed a crime. Further, the subject, in placing himself in a position to be discovered and unmasked, places the observer in the position of concealing the fact that he has seen through the subject's obfuscating efforts, and this, as already considered, renders the subject's position in the game of expression precarious indeed. Given these contingencies, the subject may find that —morality and long-range interest apart—it is simply unwise to gamble fully on concealment. Similarly, if the requirements of teamwork oblige the secret holder to share his secret, then the precariousness of the venture can be assumed to increase, and correspondingly the wisdom of not chancing conceal-ment and misrepresentation increases.[94]

The subject has an additional concern in regard to the strategic implications of play: the value of not disclosing to observers any knowledge he might have that assessment is in progress. This is a very general point and well known to those who write on military and industrial intelligence:

> By and large, for information to be power it must be secret. . . . Our business-man, whose assets include what he knows about his competitors, also has liabilities which consist of what his competitors know about him. But what he knows they know about him is not a liability; that much he can take into account in estimating and meeting competition. What he does not know that they know about him, his resources and his plans,

---

[94] And so the subject may well find it advisable not to try to cover at all. Thus, Dulles (*op. cit.*, pp. 183–184) suggests that one reason the U.S. did not find it wise to deny the Powers U-2 flight was that so many persons over the years had been required in the design, building, and operation of the U-2 that the true story would very likely reach the public if any effort at sup-pression of the general facts had been attempted.

is precisely what they can use against him, to outwit and out-maneuver him.[95]

Thus, when a subject learns that he is being secretly observed, it will usually be in his interest to conceal from his erstwhile monitor that the monitoring has been discovered.[96] An agent who is likely to be watched is advised to learn the methods which the opponent uses in keeping him under surveillance. But he should not show on any occasion that he has detected that he is being watched.[97] For presumably this can only tend to confirm for the opponent that indeed their subject has something to be wary about and that, moreover, new methods of surveillance had better be used. And the subject, of course, is likely to prefer techniques he knows about to ones that might escape him.

The value to the subject of knowing what the observer knows about him is nicely illustrated in the issue that the interrogator faces when he makes an effort to trap his subject into a useful admission. The interrogator can take the line

---

[95] Felix, op. cit., p. 38.

[96] The contemporary practice of not letting the enemy know what you know about their intended moves and resources was apparently generally extended to the treatment of discovered enemy agents just before World War I, and apparently by the English:

Quite early on, Kell [the first director of M. I. 5] made a decision which was to have far-reaching effects, and which was as important as any he ever made. After talking the matter over with Superintendent Quinn [of Scotland Yard] and getting the approval of General Ewart, Kell decided that none of the spies he had identified from Ernst's correspondence should be interfered with in any way. Only in the most extreme case of national danger would any of the German spy-ring be arrested—and even then, he laid down, nothing should be said in court which might reveal the source of the information.

By allowing the Germans to continue their activities, Kell reasoned, the headquarters in Berlin would be led to assume that the ring was unknown to the British. No effort would be made to establish another espionage organization in the country, and if war did come, it would be easy to lay hands on all the spies, by this time so familiar to the counter-espionage department. [J. Bulloch, M. I. 5 (London: Arthur Barker Ltd., 1963), p. 32] Given a net whose members don't know they are known, the possibility arises for "feeding" it incorrect information.

[97] O. Penkovskiy, The Penkovskiy Papers (New York: Doubleday, 1965), p. 124.

that he, the interrogator, already knows the facts and knows that the subject knows them, and now only waits for the subject to confirm what they both know. But as many students have suggested, this bluff has dangers that often outweigh its value. For if, in fact, in this particular, the subject is not concealing anything, or if, in fact, he knows that only he could know what the interrogator claims to know, then the subject can read from the bluff that the observer is reduced to bluffing. The whole position of the interrogator as someone close to the situation and sincere can be discredited. The subject gains the supportive knowledge that the interrogator has run out of real resources. The possibility of frightening or seducing the subject into an unwise decision is then greatly reduced. Ordinarily, then, discreditable bluffs must be avoided.[98]

The informing implications of gaming with expression—the strategic implications of the game itself—are nicely illustrated in double agentry, accounting for whatever longevity is found among those who are so employed.[99]

As suggested, an agent, once discovered, has value to his discoverers (as a means of feeding the other side false information), so long as the discovery is not discovered.

When the agent himself discovers that he has been found out, he can elect to tell his team secretly that this is the case, allowing them not only to discount the information they get but to read from it what it is the other side wants them to believe, thereby narrowing down what is likely to be true.

Or, instead, the agent can elect to face his discoverers with the discovery and offer to serve them, a situation that can also be created (and more often is) by his discoverers if they choose to tell him he has been found out and force him to work for them. The agent is thus "turned" and becomes a double agent, in this case, a "genuine" one.

---

[98] Inbau and Reid, *op. cit.*, p. 100; Mulbar, *op. cit.*, pp. 21–22, Arthur and Caputo, *op. cit.*, pp. 22–23.

[99] See, for example, Sansom, *op. cit.*, pp. 36–38.

When an agent is turned and, in addition, his original team discovers that this is so, he acquires a new strategic value for the second team, especially if he does not know that his duplicity has been discovered. He can be used to feed the opponent information known to be information they will know to be false. And as long as the opponent does not know that what they disbelieve is known to be what they disbelieve, there will be manipulative value in the transmission:

> At the end of the war, Allied Intelligence Officers discovered in captured files of the German Secret Service the text of two hundred and fifty messages received from agents and other sources before D-Day. Nearly all mentioned July and the Calais sector. One message alone gave the exact date and place of the invasion. It had come from a French colonel in Algiers. The Allies had discovered this officer was working for the Abwehr, and he was arrested and subsequently turned round. He too was used to mislead Berlin—used and abused. The Germans were so often deceived by him that they ended by treating all his information as valueless. But they kept in contact, for it is always useful to know what the enemy wants you to believe. Allied Intelligence, with great boldness and truly remarkable perversity, had the colonel announce that the Invasion would take place on the coast of Normandy on the 5th, 6th or 7th June. For the Germans, his message was absolute proof that the invasion was to be on any day *except the 5th, 6th or 7th June,* and on any part of the coast except Normandy.[100]

If the agent admits to his original team that he has been turned or if (at their direction) he allows himself to get caught just so that he can be turned, then he can be used as a "false" double agent, one who is making vulnerable those who think they have turned him. For here again he can be used to acquire false information the willing informant does not know is known to be false.

---

[100] Perrault, *op. cit.,* p. 211. Perrault adds in footnote, "The Colonel's stock with the Germans shot up after D-Day, so that the Allies were able to use him to good account for the rest of the war."

It is conceivable that a false double agent could admit his situation to the team which thought they had turned him, or be discovered by them to be a false double agent, and that there would be some value to them in receiving information that they knew was being sent to them on the assumption that they knew it was being fed to them. And in one recorded case, at least, a turned agent who admitted he had been turned, but who all the while carefully censored what he told his new masters, was known to be not playing fair and yet tolerated on the grounds that he might make a slip and reveal something.[101] But I think the game stops here, the light obtained not being worth the candle.

V THE DEGENERATION OF EXPRESSION

The more the observer suspects the subject of control, or the more he wants to guard against this possibility, the less weight he will give to the face value of the subject's behavior and the more he will seek out expressions that seem immune to fabrication and dissimulation. For the observer this can mean a heightened dependence on a special and therefore small part of the subject's expressions. However, the more the observer concentrates his interpretive effort, and the more he gambles on it, the more it will pay the subject to discover what this discovery about himself is, and control the control by extra-ordinary efforts of expression engineering. If an observer can learn about the significance of a cue, then the subject can too, and there seems no evidence that, once learned about, cannot be doctored. Uncovering moves must eventually be countered by counter-uncovering moves.

This control of uncontrollable expressions is clearly found in the case of details deemed to be so picayune in character that it is felt the subject ought to be unaware of them and hence unguarded with respect to them. For example, there

---

[101] Cookridge, *op. cit.*, p. 218.

have been parents who, returning home from an evening out, check up on their children's disavowal of having watched television by touching the top of the television set to see if it is warm. Apparently some children counter this uncovering move by cooling the set with a bag of ice cubes just after the set is turned off. The extreme example here, perhaps, is the famous Hiss-Tytell typewriter forgery.[102]

We can expect, then, the corruption of minor cues. But, of course, this corruption is also found in connection with quite substantial expressions. For example, next to waiting for a subject actually to complete his course of action, the safest plan for the observer is probably to rely on partially completed courses of action as indication of what is to come, since the more of the subject's resources that are already utilized in the beginning phases of his action, the more surely can he be counted on to follow through with his intention. And yet, of course, if the subject can be sure that the observer will take this kind of hard evidence as sufficient, then it may pay him to expend resources in this way, for their purely expressive function, however costly this may be. The famous Rothschild ploy is one example:

> In 1815, while Europe awaited news of the Battle of Waterloo, Nathan Rothschild in London already knew that the British had been victorious. In order to make a financial killing, he then depressed the market by selling British Government securities; those who watched his every move in the market did likewise, concluding that Waterloo had been lost

---

[102] In an effort to prove that Chambers could have had Hiss's Woodstock typewriter duplicated, the Hiss staff hired a typewriter expert to attempt the forgery. After working at the task for two years with the help of typeface culled from across the country, and starting only with typed pages from the original machine, Tytell produced a machine that fooled some experts. Each letter was matched for alignment, shading, defects, as well as obvious factors such as type style. Given the number of keys and the dimensions of variation it is hard to think of a more foolproof piece of evidence than a typed sheet, and therefore it is hard to think of better evidence of the scope of forgery. See M. Tytell, "The $7,500 Typewriter I Built for Alger Hiss," in K. Singer, ed., *The Secret Agent's Badge of Courage* (New York: Bemont Books, 1961), pp. 44–63.

by the British and their allies. At the proper moment he bought back in at the low, and when the news was finally generally known, the value of government securities naturally soared.[103]

Central examples come to us from the conduct of war. Thus, if the Germans are to convince the British that an underground net is intact and uninfiltrated, then it will pay to let downed flyers escape the country by means of it, for the successful management of escapes ought to be a reliable indicator of the functioning of a net.[104] How far this substantive deception can go is an interesting problem:

> A code book was found on the men [two English agents parachuted into Nazi-occupied Holland] which German counterintelligence used for two years to keep in contact with English espionage and make them believe that the messages were being sent by the Dutch partisans. Thanks to these messages, the Germans were supplied with arms and rations by the English who parachuted the goods into Holland thinking that they were being received by the partisans. To keep up this bluff, it was necessary to make the English think that the partisans were active. Thus Admiral Walter Wilhelm Canaris, head of the Abwehr, the Intelligence Bureau of OKW (German Armed Forces High Command), ordered his men to blow up four German ships anchored in the port at Rotterdam without notifying Hitler's headquarters of the order. In this way, not only the English but also the German High Command were made to think that the ships had been sabotaged by Dutch partisans (who didn't exist); and this led Hitler to order Canaris to intensify activity against the resistance groups. This was just what was needed to make the English think the partisans were active.[105]

Although this kind of showmanship may not occur frequently, nonetheless it has occurred, and often enough so as to cause

---

[103] Dulles, *op. cit.*, p. 24.

[104] Perrault, *op. cit.*, p. 207.

[105] E. Altavilla, *The Art of Spying* (Englewood Cliffs, New Jersey: Prentice-Hall), p. 21.

participants in some expression games to doubt the best of hard evidence.

It might be thought that an observer who suspected the manipulation of fugitive signs and substantive ones would have one recourse: he could perceive that the world is real, its multitude of little events in real connection with others, and that when a *multitude* of independent signs tell the same story, this can be taken for the way things are. But this belief about the meshing of facts can be exploited too. Military actions are, of course, the traditional scene of this deception in depth; moreover, just before a major invasion we can expect a diffusion and intensification of the theater of war—the real peak of the dramatic season. For example, just before D-Day the Allies apparently concerted their double agents to feed the Germans the false line that the invasion was to occur at Calais in June.[106] A German reconnaissance plane was allowed to succeed in getting over Dover harbor where it could photograph landing craft that could not make it to Normandy and therefore must be for Calais.[107] In the Dover area badly camouflaged armored divisions could be seen, but not seen well enough to tell that the equipment was made from inflated rubber.[108] Mock-up airfields and naval vessels were employed, and at the same time, real installations were camouflaged to look like barns and outbuildings.[109] Radio messages, interceptable, emanated from a headquarters in southeast England, giving the strong impression that the invasion would not be in the Normandy area; the messages, however, originated in the real headquarters and were telephoned to the false one.[110] A stand-in for Montgomery was in Gibraltar preparing to go to Africa, which argued that the major invasion was unlikely from England.[111] In Geneva "all available copies

---

[106] Perrault, *op. cit.*, p. 209.
[107] *Ibid.*, p. 192.
[108] *Ibid.*, p. 193.
[109] Dulles, *op. cit.*, p. 139.
[110] Perrault, *op. cit.*, pp. 193–194.
[111] *Ibid.*, pp. 194–196.

of Michelin map No. 51 (the Calais-Arras area) were bought up."[112] And the Calais area was bombed twice as much as the Normandy area.[113] A parallel example can be taken from another theater of war:

> In periods of high tension it is commonly accepted that deception will be an enemy tactic. Before the Pearl Harbor attack Japanese deception was very refined and ingenious. It involved, among other things, giving shore leave to large numbers of Japanese sailors, reinforcing garrisons on the northern border of Manchuria to give an impression of a thrust to the North, issuing false war plans to Japanese commanders and substituting true ones only days before the attack, and on the diplomatic side continuing the appearance of negotiation.[114]

> . . . the American naval attaché . . . informed Washington a day before the attack on Pearl Harbor that he did not expect a surprise attack because the Japanese fleet continued to be anchored at the main base of Yokosuka, as evidenced by large crowds of sailors in the streets of Tokyo. However, the naval attaché was grievously mistaken. At that very time the Japanese fleet was already well on its way to Pearl Harbor. The sailors crowding the streets of Tokyo were not sailors at all but soldiers dressed as navy men to deceive the Americans and conceal the departure of the fleet on its fateful mission.[115]

Given the corruptibility of minor cues, major cues, and meshing of cues, this follows: the more the observer relies on seeking out foolproof cues, the more vulnerable he should appreciate he has become to the exploitation of his efforts. For, after all, the most reliance-inspiring conduct on the subject's part is exactly the conduct that it would be most advantageous for him to fake if he wanted to hoodwink the observer. The very fact that the observer finds himself looking to a particular bit of evidence as an incorruptible check

---

[112] *Ibid.*, pp. 209–210.

[113] *Ibid.*, p. 193.

[114] R. Wohlstetter, "Cuba and Pearl Harbor: Hindsight and Foresight," *Foreign Affairs*, July, 1965, p. 704.

[115] Orlov, *op. cit.*, p. 2.

on what is or might be corrupted is the very reason why he should be suspicious of this evidence; *for the best evidence for him is also the best evidence for the subject to tamper with.* However many moves the observer thinks he is ahead of the subject in an expression game, he ought to feel that it is just this sense of being ahead that the subject will find of maximum use in finally trapping the observer. The harder a spy must work to obtain startling secret information, the more confidence his masters may put in his findings; but the very fact that masters do behave in this way provides the best reason why the enemy should be careful to leak false information only to those who have worked hardest to get the true facts, or insist that "turned" agents put up a show of having to work hard for the information planted with them.

Just as the observer must doubt precisely those indicators that free him from doubt (and for that reason), so the subject faces underminings too. For example, if a prospective car-buying couple wants to talk over their real feelings about how high to go in price, then they will seek out a time and place to do this safely. The salesman's "closing room," where they will be left alone while he tries to find the "manager" in order to authorize his offer, will seem admirably adapted for this strategic huddle. But the couple should suspect that not only has this room been bugged, and their deliberations monitored, but that they were steered to this room just in order to evoke and induce a relaxation of control.[116] What guides them has already guided their opponent. Similarly, if a shoplifter looks to the dressing room as a private place in which a new dress can be covered by putting her old one on over it, she will have found the place that the store management may have thought to be the best one to outfit with a one-way mirror. No doubt there are stores where it would be unnecessary for a shoplifter to worry about the dressing-room mirror, but

---

[116] Dash, Knowlton, and Schwartz, *op. cit.*, p. 212. Apparently casket-selection rooms have been bugged for the same reason. See M. Brenton, *The Privacy Invaders* (New York: Crest Books, 1964), p. 12.

today a fear on her part that the best place to steal may be the worst place is quite reasonable. And something similar can be said about high-school students who feel that the school toilet is a safe place in which to engage in various forms of illicit traffic.

A classic example of the degeneration of expression is found in the turning of intelligence agents. When, say, the British discover that one of their diplomats is a Russian spy and imprison him for forty-two years, and then five years later he escapes, what are the Russians to think? Is he their man and the information he gave them reliable? Was he all along a double agent feeding them false information and then imprisoned briefly to give false assurances that he had not been working for the British? Was he loyal to Russia but discovered by the British and, unbeknownst to himself, given false information to feed to the Russians? Has he been allowed to escape so that the Russians would wrongly think that he had really been working for the British and therefore that his information had been false? And the British themselves, to know what import the Russians gave to the spy's information, must know whether indeed the Russians think their man was really their man, and if so, whether or not this had been known from the start by the British.[117]

A final issue remains to be considered. Behind the degeneration of expression are acts of controlling, uncovering, and counter-uncovering. One can ask how far such mirroring can go? And if the play of move and countermove eventually stops, where does it stop and why does it stop when it does?

In fact, this regress seems quite limited, and for several reasons.

First, the problem for the player is to be one step ahead of the opponent, and unless the opponent is seen to be very knowing and bright, this may mean a simpler game than the player could actually sustain. This will be considered later.

[117] Altavilla, *op. cit.*, pp. 18–21.

Second, a feint can clearly be discovered to be a feint, and it then provides considerable information to the other side. (The British bizarre flare for deceit during the last war might well have backfired.) After all, if evidence of a point of invasion is either true, false, or coyly arranged to be correct but suspected, the informed enemy can at least narrow down the number of points where the invasion might occur. Similarly, although an observer may feel that the one suspect of ten who has a spotty alibi might well be innocent just because of this, it will still pay to submit him to intensive interrogation in any case. So, too, once it becomes known that the enemy knows which of one's towns have had their vital records destroyed and that an agent professing to come from there cannot easily be checked out, and once the enemy decides that the other side knows this is known, then using this town as one's own might be a good tack on the grounds that it would be appreciated that wise gamesmen wouldn't; but again, doubt once raised can be easily resolved by using other means of checking out such claimants. In the case of the late Agnes Burley, a waitress who scribbled her will on two paper napkins, the local Register of Wills set aside the attempt of surviving relatives to discredit the document, doing so on the following grounds:

> "The primitive, non-legal manner in which the will in question was written, as well as the paper towelling used, should dispute any thoughts of fraud since one desiring a deceitful end would have employed a much more formal document that would not have been scrutinized so carefully . . ." [118]

It would appear, then, that to defraud rightful heirs, one would be well advised to plant false napkins. But surely this would be an unwise maneuver. It is *possible* and even likely that a judge would give weight to such a document, but the two other possibilities must be considered also. After all, he might be insufficiently sophisticated to see that no one would

---

[118] *San Francisco Examiner and Chronicle*, April 14, 1968.

defraud in this way, and he might be so sophisticated as to suspect that a weak case has been intentionally cooked up in order to assure his belief that fraud had not occurred. In brief, once we have embarked on a course of predicting exactly how sophisticated our opponent is, the game has become chancy indeed.

Third, there will always be a fatal dilemma between the subtlety of one's miscuing and making sure that the opponent has discovered the cue in the first place. Invasion equipment is regularly camouflaged and known to be by both sides. Faked equipment badly camouflaged has been used to misdirect the enemy into thinking that they had discovered the location (with its implications) of real equipment. But surely it would be unfortunate to have to depend too much on such a ruse. It is easy to camouflage as well as one can, or so badly that it is easily evident that one was not serious; but how can one decide how well to camouflage so that the hidden object will neither be unperceived nor seen to be unseriously camouflaged?

In addition, we can expect that certain expression games will have their own natural limits. It is true that an agent will have to go through many turnings before his value is entirely used up. But once the information state is reached wherein both sides know that the other side knows that he has been turned, then, I think, the game is pretty well over—and, of course, for him, pretty well up.

Finally, there are questions of morale. Here, clearly, we face one of the limiting conditions of advanced play. To knowingly send one's own men to certain death when they are ignorant of the sacrifice they are making is an action that can weaken morale among those who make the decision or come later to learn about it. For example, during war, one side can test the reliability of its agents among the enemy by warning these spies of an impending air raid on a city, the notion being that if the agents are turned or unknowingly known then the city will be prepared and the raid unsuccessful. The other side, wanting to keep the enemy from knowing that its agents are turned or known, can certainly allow the city to be sacrificed, and this, some students of intelligence believe, has happened. But certainly the game stops somewhere near here, since there are many players who do not have the capacity to make a game out of a city or who feel that discovery of such a play would undermine the legitimacy of their administration.[119] For many, Kennedy's conduct of the Cuban Missile game was—however successful in terms of the game—a bad omen of the penetration of game attitudes into wrong places. (And yet, of course, it is precisely because such maneuvers press everyone to their limits that these moves become convincing ones and, because convincing, felt by some to be reasonable to employ and reasonable to suspect others of employing.)

There are, then, various limits to the possibility of mutual misdirection. However, these limits do not necessarily restrict the degeneration of expression; they merely establish the point at which the degeneration occurs.

Review now some of the implications of the degenerative process that has been considered. First, there is the issue of the corruption, or rather the disqualification, of innocence. The subject, in realizing that his conduct is likely to be distrustfully examined by the observer, will be concerned with the readings that might be made of it—with how it might "appear" to the other—even though, in fact, the subject is engaged in nothing he might want to conceal or modify. He may then be led to style his behavior, to cover his innocent tracks, so that likely misrepresentations will not occur. And he can feel that the more his conduct appears to be innocent (because it is), the more he has produced what a good misrepresentation would look like. Similarly, although the ob-

---

[119] There is also the limitation, as Robert Jervis has reminded me, that, should the city suffer the raid unwarned, the raiders will not know whether their agents are reliable or that they have been turned by a government willing to do anything to keep this fact a secret from the enemy.

server, at first, may be inclined to accept the subject's behavior at face value, as an unwitting move, he may feel that one can never be sure and that, in any case, the subject probably thinks that the observer is not taking conduct on trust, and, therefore, that it will not be safe to do so. In the same way, the observer may come to suspect covering actions as being actions designed to be seen through.

However, just as innocence is disqualified, so also is sophistication. As already suggested, the most useful information is also the most treacherous. And this is appreciated. It was thus, apparently, that the Germans, during World War II, were unable to believe that the spy Cicero could be getting material as good as he claimed to be getting and as good as, in fact, he was getting; they had to suspect a British plant.[120] Similarly, as a former agent suggests:

> The distinguishing line between a "plant" and the real thing is so thin that sometimes a bona fide offer is rejected for fear of a trap. One of the most valuable informants the NKVD ever had, a lieutenant-colonel of the German General Staff, was first turned down when he offered his services to the military attaché of the Soviet embassy in Berlin.[121]

In brief, when someone volunteers intelligence, how can it be known whether the offer is real or its opposite, namely an opening move in an act of misdirection and/or penetration?[122]

There is a further tightening to this entanglement. The more that is at stake for the two players, the more the subject "ought" to be motivated to dissemble and be concerned about being thought to be dissembling, and the more the observer should be suspicious. It is likely, then, that the more the players are concerned to win the game, the more precarious the

---

[120] E. Bazen, *I Was Cicero* (New York: Dell Books, 1964), p. 105.

[121] Orlov, *op. cit.*, p. 127. See also Dulles, *op. cit.*, p. 119.

[122] See, for example, Dulles, *op. cit.*, p. 119. Apparently, Penkovskiy had difficulty also, since the American officials he first appealed to feared they were being set up for a "provocation" (Penkovskiy, *op. cit.*, p. 63).

game will become, until the point is reached where everything is dependent on the outcome and no adequate means can be available for wise play. It is when little is staked that signs are reliable; it is when everything is to be entrusted that nothing (it can be thought) ought to be trusted at all.

The consequence of this degeneration of assessment is well known. The point is not that what seems to be the case comes to be questioned, but rather that a demoralizing oscillation of interpretation can result: the player will feel at one moment that he is being oversuspicious and that he should take the other at face value or, at worst, as someone who employs usual covers and, at the next, that a trap has been set for him. At one moment he can feel that he has finally hit upon indicators that can't be faked, and the next moment he can feel that this is exactly how the opponent wants him to accept these indications, and that they have been fabricated for this purpose. Appearances that are obviously innocent are the appearances a guilty expert gamesman would give. Appearances that are obviously suspect can demonstrate innocence, because no competent gamesman would allow such circumstances to arise. Yet innocence can reveal innocence and suspect appearances guilt.

In unimportant situations there is a comforting continuum, with valid appearances at one end and obviously faked ones at the other—the only difficulty being with cases in the middle. But in matters of significance, matters likely to arouse sharply opposed interests, the end of the continuum can come together to form a terrible loop. When the situation seems to be exactly what it appears to be, the closest likely alternative is that the situation has been completely faked; when fakery seems extremely evident, the next most probable possibility is that nothing fake is present.

Behind these facts of game-life I think we can detect an interesting irreversible process linking events, expressions, and communication. An event associated with a subject, but of which he is not aware, is discovered by an observer to provide valid strategic information concerning the subject. A period then occurs during which the event can be employed as a direct source of information by the observer. The event has a signal life—an unwitting move duration. Soon, however, the subject discovers that he is exposing himself through this act and begins his endeavor to manipulate matters, while at the same time the observer may begin to suspect that he can no longer trust the sign. At this point two possible careers become open for the event. It may soon become discredited as a sign of anything important and be dropped from both parties' active concern. It gets, as it were, used up. Or, under other circumstances, the subject can begin to avowedly use it to signify what the observer originally took it to signify, and the latter can come to accept the event in this new role. Expression, then, becomes transformed into communication and retains this role until reasons develop—as they are likely to—for mutual suspicion to arise, this time, however, in connection with the normative commitments of the parties to communication. And so the event again drops out of active status in the expression game between the observer and his subject, but this time through a different hole.[123]

VI   THE OBSERVER-SUBJECT MODEL

Consider now some of the general reservations that can be entertained regarding the observer-subject perspective.

In the simple model presented, one person was designated the observer or searcher and another person was located in the role of subject or concealer. However, this picture of differentiation in function was tacitly qualified. It was recognized that if the observer is to inform himself effectively it will behoove him to conceal the fact that he is doing anything more than accepting the subject at face value—else he

---

[123] A very useful analysis of international signal systems and their vicissitudes can be found in R. Jervis, *The Logic of Images in International Relations* (Princeton: Princeton University Press, 1970).

will put the latter on guard and discredit his own show of ingenuousness. This makes the observer a concealer too. Similarly, if the subject aims to conceal well then he will be advised actively to try to uncover whether or not there are suspicions concerning him; this makes him a searcher too. However, here no actual symmetry of role obtains since the points at which each player takes on a function like the other's are restricted to particular nexes in the expression game in progress.

A further qualification should be mentioned here. When a subject appreciates that an observer is attempting to break his concealings and is seeking foolproof signs of the subject's plans, capacities, and so forth, then, as already suggested, the subject is in a position to exploit these presumably fugitive or uncorruptible signs to convince the observer of what the subject desires him to believe. This is the counter-uncovering move. Given this fact, we sometimes find that a subject will not only protect his secrets in this deepened way, but also actively exploit the situation to create a profitable impression upon the observer. The very tendency for observers to be vulnerable in this way becomes the basis in its own right for the subject initiating a course of action that leads to this ulti-mate basis of control. Here we can still speak of an original observer and subject. But, in fact, the re-covering moves of the subject are not a response to the treacherousness of his situation; rather the subject himself instigates the game just in order to be in a position to make this final move.

But even these qualifications leave us with too simple a pic-ture. For purposes of analysis it is convenient to restrict ex-pression games to a contest over one item of information. In real life, however, when the observer is engaged in uncover-ing one fact regarding a subject, this subject is likely to be engaged in uncovering rather unrelated facts regarding the erstwhile observer. Pairs of players involved in one expres-sion game against each other are likely to be involved in additional games too, but this time are likely to be in reversed roles. Each seeker is therefore doubly a concealer, and each concealer is doubly a seeker.[124] Two individuals can, then, play against each other, even while playing past each other.

These various qualifications notwithstanding, I do not think that the division into two roles, observer and subject, is entirely arbitrary or that for any particular aspect of interaction it doesn't matter which of the participants is accorded which of the slots.

A second general issue. It could be argued that although expression games involve two functionally differentiated roles, the good observer must be aware of what the subject is aware of and the good subject aware of what the observer knows; and, this being so, both participants ought to have the same thing in their minds and know the other knows this. In respect to information, both players will be in the same box. The famous minimax "solution" in game theory, in fact, takes this joint information state as a condition from which to derive a stable joint decision. G. H. Mead, on different and much more moral grounds, made the same assumption about his players.

However, in many expression games, as already suggested, this assumption of full intersubjectivity is unwarranted. When a subject wants to trap an observer into wrongly imputing authenticity to a piece of manufactured evidence, his job will not be accomplished merely by putting himself in the observer's place, there using his own sophistication as a standard for predicting how the observer will respond, Mead notwithstanding. That the observer may be the more shrewd

---

[124] In some recent experimental work, Michael Argyle and his colleagues have explored some of the factors which influence a participant's sense during two-person encounters of being more the subject or more the observer, and his response to being the more visible or the less visible. The suggestion is also made that the female role inclines the performer to expect to be the subject in two-person cross-sexed encounters. (See M. Argyle *et al.*, "The Effects of Visibility on Interaction in a Dyad," *Human Relations*, 21 (1968), 3–17.) One assumption and implication of this work is that each participant is in easy reach of both the subject and observer role, various experimental conditions influencing only to a degree the choice of either.

and outguess him is obvious. It is less obvious that the subject can also lose the game because of playing it too well, as expert poker players sometimes discover. The game-theory assumption that one's opponent is exactly as smart as oneself is not a wise one in daily affairs. The subject must put a stop to the cycle of moves and countermoves at the point he thinks will be exactly one step ahead of the furthest step that the observer takes, regardless of how much more devious the subject could be, if necessary. Thus, for example, when the British planted "The Man Who Never Was" in the shore waters off Spain, they endeavored to stock the corpse's effects with domestic details which would convince the Germans that the find was genuine, but these were not necessarily details that would have convinced British Intelligence:

> You are a British Intelligence officer; you have an opposite number in the enemy Intelligence, say (as in the last war), in Berlin; and above him is the German Operational Command. What you, a Briton with a British background, think can be deduced from a document does not matter. It is what your *opposite number*, with his German knowledge and background, will think that matters—what construction that *he* will put on the document. Therefore, if you want *him* to think such-and-such a thing, you must give him something which will make *him* (and not *you*) think it. But he may be suspicious and want confirmation; you must think out what enquiries will *he* make (not what enquiries would *you* make) and give him the answers to those enquiries so as to satisfy him. In other words, you must remember that a German does not think and react as an Englishman does, and you must put yourself in his mind.[125]

Two British teams practicing against each other could probably play the game in a more elegant manner.

A final issue. Throughout this paper a two-party perspective has been taken, there being a subject with the task of managing his expressions and an observer with the task of gaining valid information. A limiting case was that of coer-

---

[125] Montagu, *op. cit.*, pp. 24–25.

cive exchange where the subject was made to act against himself. But although two-party analysis covers most of the facts, it does not cover them all. Three-party analysis is required at certain points. Take, for example, the ungentlemanly technique known as "planting." In order to substantiate his point of view, his assessment—that is, in order to cause others to assess a situation in a particular way—an observer may "plant" evidence or impute acts to a subject, so that the subject will find that he has, in effect, provided the facts that the observer was looking for. The subject, of course, is not likely to be taken in by this effort or expected to be; it is a neutral third audience that is expected to be tricked by the act. Thus, the police are often credited with leaving drugs in the room of a suspected pusher to ensure that there will be sufficient evidence to convict him. Intelligence people have been credited with mailing payments to a spy that they, in fact, have not turned, so that the spy's superiors would become suspicious. Note that the possibility of planting suggests that all along we have been making the assumption that the subject would be in charge of certain areas of the environment and be given exclusive right within that area to manage impressions as best he can against his adversary. Planting breaks this rule by entering what ought to be the subject's domain of action. The harshest expression game may nonetheless honor this rule, and usually does, since planting seems an undeveloped part of the game.

Three-party analysis, then, might open up questions that cannot be raised by looking only at an observer and a subject. Take, for example, what we have already looked at—double agentry.

To examine abstractly the dealings of a turned agent with his two masters, we must consider the nature of personal relationships and the nature of communication systems. A general statement involving all such considerations is complicated, parts of it being easier to record than to follow. To ease matters, let us temporarily give names to our parties. Call them Tom, Dick, and Mary.

Howsoever we define "personal relationship" it will be reasonable to assume that the persons related will expect a degree—whether great or small—of candor between them and that the stability of the relationship will depend upon the maintenance of this condition. (In this way, personal relationships provide a social basis for a communication channel, and a communication channel becomes one of the defining attributes of a relationship.)

The personal relationship between Tom and Dick is given stability when nothing Dick can discover about Tom's belief in what he tells Dick can alter Dick's willingness to accept these statements at face value, as self-believed ones. Tom, in brief, can handle his communications so as to render himself undiscreditable, albeit not necessarily always correct. On the other side are circumstances which make for instability: Tom can attempt to mislead Dick with self-disbelieved statements presented as self-believed ones. Here disruptive discovery is possible, that is, a disclosure which will threaten the understanding between Dick and Tom as to Tom's candor. Note that in stable arrangements Tom may hold back information from Dick, providing he does not conceal that he is holding it back, and providing that this lack of openness has already been accepted as part of the relationship.

A completely stable relation between Tom and Dick in either, let alone both, directions is not, in real life, ordinarily possible. For one thing, each person will owe the other tactful expression of beliefs regarding negatively valued attributes of the other. Nonetheless individuals often do make an effort to ensure what stability they can. Tom may well chance discrepancies between what he says and what he himself believes providing he alone possesses the discreditable information. On the other hand, discrepancies over whose disclosure he has incomplete control he may wish to avoid at all cost. And so there is the technique of "filling in," whereby Tom voluntarily divulges to Dick whatever information is necessary to protect Tom from the possibility of Dick learning elsewhere what Tom will prove to have been in a position to tell

Dick himself, and ought to have told, given their relationship. All of this has been implied in the comments on interrogation.

When Tom communicates to Mary he will again have various reasons for censoring what he says, as was the case in his management of Dick, except that now Tom will feel obliged to censor a different set of opinions, among which will be those pertaining to his evaluation of Mary. It can come to pass, then, that Tom divulges to Mary information that has the power to discredit or disrupt the line he maintains to Dick. Now, if Mary and Dick are in communication, Mary will find herself in an interestingly delicate position. At any one moment two courses of communicative action are open to her. She can refrain from telling Dick what she knows, but he does not, about Tom's opinions of him. This, in effect, puts her in a collusive relation with Tom against Dick, and, in turn, gives her power over Tom—the power to embarrass his relation to Dick. The other course of action available to Mary is for her to divulge to Dick Tom's secrets from Dick. This transforms the relations among the triad as follows: Mary's relation to Tom is placed in jeopardy. If Dick tells Tom what Mary has disclosed, then her relation to Tom is undercut. During the period that Dick does not make this disclosure, he finds himself with a double power. As suggested, he has power over Mary to undercut her relation to Tom. (This is what makes the job of intelligence officer touchy; to recruit agents he must expose himself to persons who have no reason yet to protect his discreditable relation to civil society.) And Dick will also have a kind of power over Tom—the kind that comes from Tom having to maintain a line to Dick that Tom doesn't know is no longer convincing.

Note that what has been said here about Tom, Dick, and Mary can equally be said about Dick, Tom, and Mary and the four other combinations of these three actors. Moreover, there seems to be a tendency for this daisy chaining to occur, with every member of the triad in the power of every other member, and every member in a collusive relation with every other member. There may even be a certain stability to such an interlocking of unstable communication relations because of the multiplicity of checks—everyone, in effect, is in a position to blackmail everyone else.[126]

In general, however, one can expect that triads, like dyads, will have some instability. Because of this, there is sometimes to be found the practice of "clearing the channels"—that is, a special effort is made by one participant—say, Tom—to make sure that his relation to neither Dick nor Mary can be undercut by a divulgence from the other. To do this, Tom tells each what he tells the other, and also tells each that he has told the other. Of course, Tom would then still find himself with entrusted secrets of Dick's (which Mary would like to know about), and entrusted secrets of Mary's (which Dick would like to know about). A complete clearing of the network is found when each of the three participants clears his own channels. It might be added that the longer the life of the triad, and the more matters of concern the members share, the more likely is the system to be unstable, or stable for unpleasant reasons, and, perhaps, the more the members yearn for a time when matters were less sticky.

VII   CONCLUSIONS

It is certainly the case that nations at war (and is likely the case that industrial organizations at peace) have been wonderfully served by effective spies; Sorge and Cicero are only two examples. But just as certainly, the overall value of intelligence organizations of the national kind can be questioned.[127]

The more needful an organization is of acquiring or guarding a piece of information, the more it must suspect the

[126] Kathleen Archibald suggests that friendship triads (and more extended networks) can be stabilized in other ways, too: Tom can, in regard to his negative feelings about Dick, be more candid to Dick than he is to Mary. If Dick and Mary also follow this policy, the triad is stabilized.

[127] Here see H. Wilensky, *Organizational Intelligence* (New York: Basic Books, 1967).

employee associated with it, for that is just the time when the opponent will make the greatest effort to get to him. Officers in the home establishment can be subverted through ideology, blackmail, bribery, and carelessness. One's agents in enemy lands are even more vulnerable. They can easily be caught without this being known, and bribed with their lives into working for the other side. (Even if this requires that they not be trusted out of the sight of their new masters, they can still be used, since a considerable amount of a wartime agent's work consists in receiving and sending messages and arranging to receive agents and supplies.)

For an intelligence organization, rationalization in the conventional sense generates special vulnerabilities, and growth special weaknesses. Hierarchical organization means that one man "in place" near the top can render the whole establishment vulnerable. In the field, lateral expansion through links means that one caught spy can lead to the sequential entrapment of a whole network.[128] In both cases, the damage that can be done by a disloyal member is multiplied. The usual answer is compartmental insulation and minimization of channels of communication. But these devices, in turn, reduce coordination of action and dangerously impede corroboration of information.

Behind the instability of intelligence organization, I think we can find two fundamental facts. First, much of the work of the organization ultimately depends on guarding information the other side is seeking. (This is directly true of the security branch and indirectly true for the espionage branch, the latter simply because agents can't uncover other organizations' secrets without maintaining secrecy concerning their attempts.) And among all the things of this world, information is the hardest to guard, since it can be stolen without

---

[128] The classic case here was the breaking of the British code and security signal for Dutch agents in 1941 by the Germans and the eventual establishment of 17 false radio links with Britain along with the capture of all agents sent during a three-year period. See Cookridge, *op. cit.*, pp. 390ff.; also H. Giskes, *London Calling North Pole* (London: Kimber, 1953).

removing it. Second, in working with information, individuals must be employed, and of all the capacities that an individual has, that of being a caretaker of information is one that seems to render him most vulnerable. Hence intelligence work and intelligence workers provide much material on the playing of expression games. It is here we can see most clearly the contingencies a member creates for a social organization by virtue of his actual capacity as a source and manager of information. And it is here we can most easily learn about the beliefs which prevail concerning the moral and practical limits of this capacity.

A final point. It is plain that the experience of intelligence agents—more so the popular recountings of the supposed experiences of intelligence agents—might provide an overly colorful source of data on which to base an analysis of expression games. Nonetheless, I think there is some warrant for using this literature. Intelligence agents, especially from the larger countries, have considerable resources at their disposal, a certain amount of specialized training, a government's secret blessing to commit mayhem, and stakes that are very high. In these respects agents are unlike ordinary mortals. But along with everyone else, they must make their peace with one massive contingency: the player's chief weapon and chief vulnerability is himself. Getting oneself through an international incident involves contingencies and capacities that have a bearing on the games that go on in local neighborhoods. For example, the very great Russian spy, Sorge, after having maneuvered himself into the position of unofficial secretary to the German military attaché in Tokyo, found it necessary to photograph documents in Embassy rooms in which he could easily have been surprised at work.[129] Being caught once in such an act in such a place would have rather dramatically altered his working identity. Yet he was able coolly to proceed with his work and his risk-taking. What is

---

[129] F. Deakin and G. Storry, *The Case of Richard Sorge* (New York: Harper & Row, 1966), p. 181.

special here is the place, the equipment, and the consequences of discovery. But these are special only in degree. At the center is a man having to engage in a complex technical act over a brief period of available time under conditions where the chances of discovery by others, with consequent exposure and discrediting, are considerable; and he must execute his technical task without allowing thoughts of his situation to reduce his effective speed—for this would only increase time, risk, and fear, which, in turn, could lead to still further incapacity. We all must face moments of this kind, albeit much less extreme in every regard, and it is the sharing of this core contingency that makes the stories of agents relevant. Similarly, to hide bulky transmitter and receiver parts in a rucksack while ostensibly going on a hike,[130] or to regularly meet with a member of one's spy ring in his own house under cover of giving painting lessons to his daughter,[131] or to pass a vital message to a confederate during the act of shaking hands with a member of another embassy at a cocktail party, is to engage in spectacular concealment; but there is no one who does not have to orient his body's covering as a means of concealing something, or who has not used ordinary arrangements of social contact as a front behind which to engage in questionable dealings, or who has not fabricated a "good" reason for actions that spring from a concealed intent. It is an unusual feat, even in espionage, for a man to move "into place" and stay in play for fourteen years, establishing a social reputation as a watch repair proprietor so that he could make his move when needed, as indeed "Albert Oertal" did; [132] but there is no one who has not gone somewhere for reasons he did not want to avow and protected himself by providing "good" reasons for his visit. It is mainly wanted criminals, spies, and secret police

---

[130] *Ibid.*, p. 207.

[131] *Ibid.*, p. 215.

[132] A version can be found in K. Singer, *Spies Who Changed History* (New York: Ace Books, 1960), pp. 140–147.

who must extendedly present themselves in a false personal and/or social identity to those who think they know them well; but there can hardly be a person who has never been concerned about giving his social or personal identities away, whether through lack of emotional and intellectual self-control, or the failure to inhibit expression, or the acknowledgment of a social relationship he was not supposed to have, or the demonstration of incongruous social practices.

And note, just as we are like them in significant ways, so they are like us. In the little service contacts we have in stores and offices, occasions are always arising when we must ask for advice and then determine how to read the advice by trying to analyze the sincerity of the server's manner. When we come into contact with the person who employs us, a similar task arises; he has reason to almost cover his actual assessment with an equable, supporting air, and we have reason to try to read his for what he "really" thinks. The same is true in the warmer circles of social life. Surely every adult who has had a friend or spouse has had occasion to doubt expression of relationship and then to doubt the doubt even while giving the other reasons to suspect that something is being doubted. These, then, are the occasions for our expression games, but a nation's gamesmen play here too. He who manages the affairs of state has to make fateful decisions on the basis of the appearances of good faith of those with whom he negotiates; similarly, an intelligence officer is dependent on being able to appraise correctly the show of loyalty displayed by his agents.

In every social situation we can find a sense in which one participant will be an observer with something to gain from assessing expressions, and another will be a subject with something to gain from manipulating this process. A single structure of contingencies can be found in this regard which renders agents a little like us all and all of us a little like agents.

81

Strategic
Interaction

Strategic Interaction

Whenever students of the human scene have considered the dealings individuals have with one another, the issue of calculation has arisen: When a respectable motive is given for action, are we to suspect an ulterior one? When an individual supports a promise or threat with a convincing display of emotional expression, are we to believe him? When an individual seems carried away by feeling, is he intentionally acting this way in order to create an effect? When someone responds to us in a particular way, are we to see this as a spontaneous reaction to the situation or a result of his having canvassed all other possible responses before deciding this one was the most advantageous? And whether or not we have such concerns, ought we to be worried about the individual believing that we have them?

In recent years this traditional concern about calculation has been taken up and refined by students of game theory. This paper attempts to isolate the analytical framework implied in the game perspective, and show its relationship to other perspectives in analyzing interpersonal dealings.

I

Individuals typically make observations of their situation in order to assess what is relevantly happening around them and what is likely to occur. Once this is done, they often go on to exercise another capacity of human intelligence, that of making a choice from among a set of possible lines of re-

85

sponse. Here some sort of maximization of gain will often be involved, often under conditions of uncertainty or risk. This provides one sense in which an actor is said to be "rational," and also an ethically neutral perspective from which to make judgments concerning the desirability and advisability of various courses of action. *Rational decision-making* is involved.

Obviously, both assessment and decision-making depend on related capacities of intelligence, such as storing experience of events and making this experience available when it is relevant. However, whose interests are served by an individual's intelligence is quite another matter, an understanding of which requires a shift from psychological to social terms.

The kind of entity this paper will be concerned with can be called a *party,* to be defined as something with a unitary interest to promote. By the term *coalition* is meant a joining of two or more, ordinarily opposed, parties, and their functioning, temporarily and in regard to specific aims, to promote a single interest .

The interests of a party are promoted by action taken on the party's behalf by individuals who are authorized to act for it and are capable of doing so. An individual agent is called a *player* (or sometimes, an "actor"). The player exercises human intelligence, assessing "his" party's situation, selecting from the available courses of action and committing his party to this selection. Note that an individual may simultaneously play for a party and—in another of his relevant capacities—be part of the party itself, as every executive with a stock option knows. Moreover, the individual often acts for a party of which he himself is the acknowledged sole member; in poker (but not in bridge) we usually expect that the individual will "play for himself." [1] The analytical differences be-

---

[1] Personal documents about religious asylums and radical political movements suggest an opposite possibility, namely, that an individual can voluntarily renounce his will, take on the "armor of obedience," and actively embrace curtailments of what he would ordinarily consider to be his self-

tween party and player can here become easy to neglect, as I shall sometimes.

The game-theoretical approach is clear enough on the need to divide the individual into party and player, but less clear about other distinctive ways in which the individual can function in the gaming situation. He can serve as a *pawn*. I mean here that conditions can be such as to place in jeopardy the social or bodily welfare of an individual, and this welfare can be the interest that is at stake in the game.[2] Now it should be seen that although this kind of welfare is obviously an attribute of the individual in jeopardy, a concern to preserve this state may well be the interest of a friend, a family, or even a tribe. It is so when an infant is given or taken as a hostage, or when pursuit is dampened because the owners of a car have been forced to ride along with the gunmen who are stealing it.

An individual may also function as a *token,* that is, a means of expressing and marking openly a position that has been taken. The early history of Western diplomacy recognized this possibility with a term, *nuncio,* to refer to someone who had the capacity to substitute for the presence of his principal, that is, his party, although not to negotiate for it. (A *procurator*, on the other hand, could negotiate but not ceremonially represent, being a player solely.)[3] Private life provides its own ceremonial example: When an individual decides to pay his respects to an acquaintance, different ceremonial forms may be open to him. He can send a telegram, leave his card, cause flowers to be delivered, or make a personal visit.

---

interests. Militancy of this kind can thus be seen as a game the individual plays against himself. A minor domestic version is found in self-discipline techniques: an individual who is his strong-minded self while shopping does not allow himself to buy favorite sweet foods, knowing that at home there will be times when he will be his weak-minded self.

[2] For example, it is said that family members of Soviet officials touring the United States were sometimes kept at home to insure return in good faith by the traveler. See S. de Gramant, *The Secret War* (New York: Dell, 1963), p. 194.

[3] G. Mattingly, *Renaissance Diplomacy* (London: Jonathan Cape, 1955), p. 30.

All these forms can be functionally equivalent, each constituting a valid mark of regard; in the last case, however, the individual uses himself as a token in the ceremony.

I have mentioned several functions of the individual in the version of interaction we are to consider. One further function must be considered that will later much concern us. Obviously, the individual can serve as a source of information which others can use in arriving at their assessment of the situation. Thus, we fully assume that important hiring is likely to involve a "personal interview," and that important dates will not be blind. We can also assume that our British allies can more easily recruit nationals to spy on us than can our Japanese friends.

A party, then, can use an individual as a player, pawn, token, and informant. In each of these cases, the individual serves as a special kind of game-relevant resource. But of course the individual can also function as a less differentiated and less special resource: someone who performs a prescribed instrumental task with no necessary self-awareness of the value of this task for furthering the interests of the party, and no appreciable discretion in executing the performance. A gunner is a part, however small, of the striking capability of a commander, but in the same sense as is the gun that is assigned to him.

Given the several ways in which the individual can perform, we must expect to find these functions often overlayed upon each other. An individual who functions as a pawn need not, of course, participate in any other capacity, being "innocently involved," as we say; but just as clearly, he who functions as a pawn can also be the player, as the story of Judith tells us.[4] Our modern term "ambassador," to take another ex-

---

[4] Daughter of Merari, widow of Menasses and very beautiful to behold. Her city, under siege, was cut off from water by the armies of Assyria under their chief captain, the invincible Holofernes, causing her people to begin to doubt that the Lord looked after them. Judith devised and executed the plan of going forth from the walls of the city into the valley unto the watch of the enemy, and from there, by the wit and guile known to her sex, into

STRATEGIC INTERACTION

ample, combines the functions of the earlier roles of *nuncio*
and *procurator*. Similarly, he who functions as both pawn and
player can also function as the party—the complication routinely found in sexual seductions and duels. Note finally that
although an individual can function as a pawn or as a token,
other objects of concern and value can also, and, more typically than individuals, do. The player function, on the other
hand, is largely restricted to individuals, the doomsday machine being one of the exceptions.

II

Given the elements that have been defined, one can now
go on to consider their interactions. For this it will be useful
to follow a custom in game theory and employ miniature
scenarios of a very farfetched kind.

Our hero, Harry the forest ranger, is caught in a brush fire
and perceives that to his right there is a tall tree that might
be possible to climb and may survive the flames, and to his
left a high bridge already beginning to burn.

Harry here is party, player, and pawn. As a party he has
an interest to save a life. As a player he assesses the situation
and tries to dope out the best chances. As a pawn, he is the
life that is in jeopardy.

Harry's situation is such that four distinctive courses of
action seem open to him. He can make for the bridge. He can
make for the tree. He can call on his gods to save him. He can
dither, that is, tentatively try to discover new outs, vacillate
between bridge and tree, or give way to screams, rantings,
and fainting. I shall use the word *turn* to refer to Harry's

---

the tent of Holofernes, and from there, after three days to entrance him, into
his heart and alone by his side. While thusly placed she cut off his head,
and by night stole with it and her maid back to her people, the object
being to renew their confidence in God's care by a display of her winnings.
Tradition has it that although Holofernes used Judith well, not having de-
filed her, she used him better. No mention is made that for such a nice
girl, Judith showed a certain want of feeling, but then, of course, Holofernes
was not a Jewish boy.

moment and opportunity for choice, and *move* to refer to the action he takes consequent on deciding to play his turn now.[5]

In dealing with his situation, Harry can take a disinterested gamelike approach. He can list all his possibilities, attach a success probability function to each, and solve his problem by selecting what seems to be his best chance. This itself may not be a simple matter. The probability that the bridge will burn before he gets across it must be considered against the chances of surviving the high fall into the water. In any case, one has here something that can be defined as a game against nature, even though it might be thought that, for a full-fledged game to occur, Harry must have a human opponent.[6]

Although a game against nature is a rudimentary game indeed, some concepts important to game analysis can be introduced by it. One of these is the *move*. A move, analytically speaking, is not a thought or decision or expression, or anything else that goes on in the mind of a player; it is a course of action which involves real physical consequences in the external world and gives rise to objective and quite concrete alterations in Harry's life situation. (This fact is sometimes obscured because of the unfortunate role of recreational board games in the discussion of gaming.) Furthermore, a

---

[5] The distinction is von Neumann's, but the language, which is in line with everyday usage, is not. What he calls a choice, I call a move; what he calls a move, I call a turn.

[6] There are, of course, games and games.

In game theory, the term game tends to be used (as it will be here) to refer to a single decision-requiring situation structured in certain ways, or at most, a brief sequence of contingent moves.

Everyday usage derives from recreational board games. These provide for a special kind of unserious activity whose features should not be confused with those of concern to game theory. Board games are often played for fun with no obvious connection with the surrounding world; they are nicely bounded in time and place; there is great consensus concerning their rules; the game counters have little value except when part of a game in action; the moves are extremely interdependent, and the interlocking of fate (albeit game fate) is extensive; zero-sum conditions usually prevail; very extended sequences of contingent moves are involved, so much so that in a game like chess a complete ("pure") strategy is practically unthinkable.

Recently in popular psychiatric literature, the term game has been employed as a loose but stylish substitute for tactic, "ploy," or "mechanism."

move is a course of action chosen from a small number of radically different alternative ones in the situation.[7] And this situation itself is one that presents Harry with an urgent predicament and a highly structured, nicely bounded setting in which he must face this predicament. In such a clarifying setting, a course of action becomes a move. In fact, in this setting, no action at all on Harry's part can have fully serious, clear-cut consequences and hence constitute a move "in effect." Finally, one can here treat Harry as a gamesman because his situation is such as to make this kind of schematic analysis realistic.

So far Harry, our hero, has been little involved in social matters, except where he draws on cultural lore about bridges and trees, or upon his Keds in order to run fast and be surefooted. But the scene can easily be changed so that the implacable natural environment is more man-made. Put goggles on Harry and put him high in the sky in a single-seater. Harry, the pilot, begins to lose altitude due to engine trouble. He must jump with a faulty parachute that might not open, or try to bring the plane down, or dither. (I am assuming here that Harry doesn't have a prayer in spite of improved reception.)

A point about ends and means can now be raised. The choice between life and death as values seems so automatic that we may feel that the only issue is to select the best means. But preference always enters the question in an additional way. If parachuting is to mean that a very costly experimental plane will, for sure, crash in a densely populated area, then Harry as a player will have to decide just whom he is playing for, himself or the community, and this indeed may not be an automatic decision. The question here is not so much that of the "intersubjective comparison of utility," as is often assumed, but simply that of a player deciding which of

---

[7] There is some difference of opinion concerning the necessity of this particular assumption. See, for example, R. Braithwaite, *Theory of Games as a Tool for the Moral Philosopher* (Cambridge: Cambridge University Press, 1963), pp. 71–76.

two parties he is playing for. It should be added that, ordinarily, it is assumed that Harry's interest in saving his own life doesn't need an explanation, but that his willingness to put others ahead of himself does. In truth, however, if the game framework alone is assumed, both kinds of concern on a player's part are equally difficult to explain.[8]

In the plots so far, Harry has been exposed to a blind and blunt nature, remodeled in various degrees by man. Let us now invest the danger to Harry in a force to which he is not only *exposed* but also *opposed,* thus rendering his situation more gamey. Harry, the hunted, has spotted, but has not been spotted by, a hungry-looking lion, and only one nearby tree seems high enough to offer possible protection. Harry can make a dash for it, exposing his presence, and try to get to and up the tree before he is cut off; he can freeze and hope to go unseen or prove uninteresting. (I assume that by now Harry knows enough neither to dither nor pray.)

Let us now note that Harry, in considering the merits of making a dash for it, must weigh the fact that a race for the tree necessarily exposes him to the lion as an edible moving object, and may even expose his intention, depending on the intelligence of his royal adversary. Being visible to the lion is an important part of Harry's situation. Visibility is not an incidental part of the tree move, superimposed, as it were, but rather a basic feature of the move itself. If Harry could find a concealed path to the tree, he would find an entirely different move. Similarly, the nature of freezing, as a move, is inextricably tied up with the fact that Harry frozen has a possibility of remaining of no concern to the lion.

---

[8] Similarly, when students consider the Meadian notion that during interaction the individual is obliged to take the attitude of the other, they tend to take for granted that the individual will also be required to take his own point of view, too, else an acceptable playing out of behavior will not be possible. Since it is "natural" to take one's own point of view, the only problem that appears to exist is to account for taking the view of the other. Here see M. Feffer and L. Suchotliff, "Decentering Implications of Social Interaction," *Journal of Personality and Social Psychology,* 4 (1966), 415–422.

It will be noted that if the lion is given full credit, he can be defined as a party with an intentioned interest, the eating of Harry, and that this interest is, of course, directly opposed to Harry's, which is not to be eaten. Further, the lion can be expected to track Harry, to pursue him, whereas a forest fire would not (a guided missile, of course, could). Finally, there is a hint of the possibility that the lion could, at least "in effect," read Harry's intentions as well as his presence, and, should Harry make for the tree, try to cut him off by running for the tree, not for Harry. Harry, in short, is faced not merely by an inimical force but by an opponent.

All of this can be seen more clearly if we complete the transition to a fully gamelike situation.

Harry, the native spearsman, having strayed from the territory populated by his tribesmen, comes into a small clearing to find that another spearsman from a hostile tribe is facing him from what would otherwise be the safe side. Since each finds himself backed by the other's territory, retreat is cut off. Only by incapacitating the other can either safely cross the clearing and escape into his own part of the forest.

Now the game. If there were no chance of missing a throw, then the first spearsman to throw would win. However, the likelihood of missing a fixed target increases with the distance of the throw. In addition, a throw, as a move, involves a spear easily seen to be on its way by its target. And the target itself isn't quite fixed. It is able to dodge and will certainly try to do so. The greater the distance of the throw, the more time to dodge it and the greater the chance of doing so. (A poison dart silently shot from a concealing bush is a move, too, but one that does not telegraph its puncture, and hence, of course, one that generates quite a different game.) And to miss a throw while the other still has his spear allows the other to approach at will for an easy win. Thus, each player begins at a point where it does not pay to chance a throw and presumably approaches a point where it does not pay not to. And each player, in deciding what to do, must decide knowing the other is engaged in exactly the same sort of decision, and knowing that they both appreciate this.

Now return for a moment to Harry the fire ranger, pilot, and hunted. He explores possible courses of action by trying them out in his mind. To do this he must put himself in the situation of a fire, a plane, or a lion as much as his knowledge and human limitations allow. When, however, Harry's opponent is neither animal nor mineral but a competent gamester in his own right—then the "doping out" function changes considerably. Harry will find much more scope for his empathy since the other is a something like himself. (And yet note that we have still not dealt with verbal communication or even with well-established mutually recognized signals; we have dealt only with a more elementary process—assessment of the situation.)

Harry, then, will be concerned (and able) to make an assessment of his opponent's situation. The game-theoretical approach suggests a way of describing the other's situation in well-structured terms, in this case, the features of the other's situation that Harry is likely to want to know about.

Obviously, the first matter for Harry to consider is the other's moves. A series of possibilities will have to be considered. Least important, perhaps, are "decisions," namely moves that the opponent has decided to undertake, but has, so far, done nothing about implementing. (Of course, here Harry will have to give weight to many factors: the logical impossibility of ever knowing, for sure, what a party's intentions are; the opponent's record in following through with his intentions; the likelihood of the opponent knowing that his intention is known, and hence concluding that he must alter his plans; etc.) More important are readied moves and begun ones—those that the opponent has prepared and started to commit his resources to and therefore has a game-worthy reason for completing. Discovery of these moves before the final playing out of the game is crucial. Classic examples are found in military affairs—for example, the discovery of enemy gas shells, plans for their use against one's own side, and identification of the gas—all in time to perfect a neutralizing agent and to equip one's own men with gas masks. Finally, there are moves which the opponent has actually executed or accomplished but which Harry, up to now, has not discovered.[9] The Russian missiles in Cuba were almost an example.

A second matter that Harry will want to know about is what has been called *operational code*,[10] namely, the orientation to gaming that will diffusely influence how the opponent plays. Here several factors must be considered. There is the opponent's preference pattern or utility function, namely, his ordering, weak or strong, of aims and goals. There are his normative constraints, the self-imposed conditions on furthering his objectives he is likely to observe for reasons of moral sentiment or conscience.[11] And a residual category: *style of play*.[12]

Next to consider is *resolve*, that is, the opponent's determination to proceed with the game at whatever price to himself. Resolve, of course, is to be considered relative to a particular game and is not solely a function of the opponent's resoluteness, that is, his general tendency to persevere or not in whatever game he is playing.

Also, it will be useful for Harry to know about the other's *information state*. I refer here to the knowledge the opponent may possess about the important features of his own situation and of Harry's. For example, if Harry plans to deceive the

---

[9] R. Seth, *Anatomy of Spying* (New York: Dutton, 1963), pp. 62–64. Note that what is a readied move from the perspective of one game can be (where getting ready is defined as the goal) an accomplished move from the perspective of another.

[10] N. Leites, *The Operational Code of the Politburo* (New York: McGraw-Hill, 1951). See also R. Benedict, *The Chrysanthemum and the Sword* (New York: Houghton Mifflin, 1946), "The Japanese in the War," ch. 2, pp. 20–42.

[11] Norms are often considered, but I think quite wrongly, as part of preference pattern. The utility concept can certainly be stretched in this way, but then it covers everything.

[12] Relevant material can be found in L. Haimson, "The Soviet Style of Chess," in M. Mead and R. Metraux, eds., *The Study of Culture at a Distance* (Chicago: Chicago University Press, 1953), pp. 426–431; T. Uesugi, and W. Vinache, "Strategy in a Feminine Game," *Sociometry*, 26 (1963), 75–78, and L. Wylie, *Village in the Vaucluse* (New York: Harper & Row, 1964), "Boules," pp. 250–259.

other, it will be important for Harry to know what the other suspects or expects, for these beliefs will provide the lines along which he can be misled.[13]

A further matter for Harry to consider is the opponent's *resources* or capacities—the stuffs that the other *as a party* can draw upon in his adaptations to the situation. (Harry's own resources will be important to him too, of course.)

Now a central resource of the other as a party is his having someone to play for him. And given that the other has a player, in this case the other himself, it is important for Harry to know something about the attributes of this player. (Thus, when a mental hospital psychiatrist deals with a patient who is new to him, the patient's dossier will be a useful thing to examine beforehand, as is true also when diplomats, friendly or hostile, deal with each other, except here *all* the participants are likely to have had access to dossiers on the others.) [14]

Perhaps the most important attribute of players is their *gameworthiness*. I include here: the intellectual proclivity to assess all possible courses of action and their consequences, and to do this from the point of view of all the contesting parties; the practice of setting aside all personal feelings and all impulsive inclinations in assembling the situation and in following a course of action; the ability to think and act under pressure without becoming either flustered or transparent; the capacity to refrain from indulging in current displays of wit and character at the expense of long-term interests; [15]

---

[13] A. Dulles, *The Craft of Intelligence* (New York: Signet Books, 1964), p. 136.

[14] See, for example, C. Thayer, *Diplomat* (New York: Harpers, 1959), p. 15.

[15] H. Nicolson, *Diplomacy* (New York: Oxford University Press, 1964), pp. 63–64, suggests:

A diplomatist . . . is not an ideal diplomatist unless he be also modest. The dangers of vanity in a negotiator can scarcely be exaggerated. . . . It may cause him to offend by ostentation, snobbishness or ordinary vulgarity. It is at the root of all indiscretion and of most tactlessness. It lures its addicts into displaying their own verbal brilliance, and into such fatal diplomatic indulgences as irony, epigrams, insinuations, and the barbed reply.

and, of course, the ability and willingness to dissemble about anything, even one's own capacities as a gamesman. Not surprisingly, the literature on diplomacy stresses these gamesman qualities, since diplomats may have to represent parties of great importance in situations where minor interaction gains can have great consequences:

> There are some additional qualifications necessary, in the practical part of business, which may deserve some consideration in your leisure moments—such as, an absolute command of your temper, so as not to be provoked to passion upon any account; patience, to hear frivolous, impertinent, and unreasonable applications; with address enough to refuse, without offending; or by your manner of granting, to double the obligation;—dexterity enough to conceal a truth, without telling a lie; sagacity enough to read other people's countenance; and serenity enough not to let them discover anything by yours— a seeming frankness, with a real reserve. These are the rudiments of a politician; the world must be your grammar.[16]

Another important attribute of players is their *integrity*, that is, the strength of their propensity to remain loyal to a party once they have agreed to play for it, and not to instigate courses of action on behalf of some other party's interests, notably their own. One is concerned here with the "conflict of interests" problem, with normative constraints, but constraints that pertain not to parties in interaction but to intraparty elements. (Coalition formation, strictly speaking, is not at question here; the issue is not that of two parties coming into an unanticipated temporary secret joining of forces, but rather that of a player coming into a corrupted relation to his erstwhile party.[17] The diplomatic corps provides many examples, as in the use of the diplomatic pouch to smuggle in drugs destined for illegal sale, or scarce goods destined for the black

---

[16] *Letters of Lord Chesterfield to His Son*, Everyman's ed. (New York: Dutton, 1929), p. 41.

[17] It should be admitted that it is sometimes very hard indeed to distinguish between properties of players and certain properties of parties, such as resolve, normative constraint, etc.

market.[18] Less clear-cut are examples from the business world, where the right of a company executive to buy or sell stocks for his personal account on the basis of early information about the company's prospects is disputed by some publics and condoned by others.[19] Of course, if the analysis is fine enough, the issue of integrity and loyalty can occasionally become quite unclear, as Sir Harold Nicolson suggests:

> The professional diplomatist is governed by several different, and at times conflicting, loyalties. He owes loyalty to his own sovereign, government, minister and foreign office; he owes loyalty to his own staff; he owes a form of loyalty to the diplomatic body in the capital where he resides; he owes [in Sir Harold's case] loyalty to the local British colony and its commercial interests, and he owes another form of loyalty to the government to which he is accredited and to the minister with whom he negotiates.[20]

Finally, it should be stressed that if an issue cannot arise as to the integrity of an individual, then he cannot really function as a player at all, although he may form an important part of the mere or instrumental resources of a party. For example, in preparation for D-Day, the Allies apparently employed two commandos to take landing-soil samples at many points along the French coast, including the five beaches that were to be used. Each of the samplings subjected the two men to very considerable risk, but this risk was considered to be worth the obfuscation provided by the multiple locations of the samples. Further, it was felt that should the men be captured and interrogated, they them-

---

[18] See Thayer, *op. cit.*, p. 41.

[19] See, for example, "Bonanza Trouble: SEC vs. Texas Gulf Raises Sticky Question," *Life* (Aug. 6, 1965), pp. 29–37.

[20] Nicolson, *op. cit.*, p. 65. Nicolson (pp. 34–35) also comments on the complications introduced into judgments regarding the obligations of representatives when, during their residency abroad, there is a radical change in administration at home. Robert Jervis suggests that even when a diplomat does have a stable home audience he can still appear to lack integrity because of being exposed to sources of information and impression different from those available to his masters.

selves would not be able to divulge the landing points since they themselves would not have been placed in a situation in which they could surmise the truth.[21] Had the men risked their lives only on the beaches that were to be used, they would have been players in the D-Day game; as it was, they were merely resources.

These, then, are the game-defined elements of the opponent's situation. But of course, the game-theoretical approach has something else to say about the assessment that Harry makes of his opponent. Clear recognition is given to the fact that the opponent's assessment of his own situation is an important part of his situation and that human assessments are exactly the sort of thing that Harry can try to fully penetrate and appreciate. This leads to the famous recursive problem. Harry must come to terms with the fact that the assessment he is trying to penetrate, namely, the one that the other is likely to make, will contain as one of its features the fact that Harry will try to penetrate it. Thus, the opponent that Harry must try to dope out is another that is known to himself and to Harry as someone trying to dope out Harry and someone whom Harry is trying to dope out. (Lest we give our lion too much credit, it should be noted that while the lion may, in effect, exploit slight cues to dope out Harry's intended move, the lion could hardly be neurotic enough to be concerned with the effects of Harry doping out that his dashing for the tree would likely be doped out by the lion.) This mutual appreciation constitutes a special type of assessment, the very nub of gaming, but assessment it is, not communication, although one might want to call it communication in effect, or "tacit communication," as does Schelling in brilliantly developing its role in "games of coordination." [22]

Once Harry sees the need to assess his opponent's view of the situation, game theory gives him a way of being system-

---

[21] G. Perrault, *The Secrets of D-Day* (London: Barker, 1965), p. 20.

[22] T. C. Schelling, *The Strategy of Conflict* (Cambridge: Harvard University Press, 1960), pp. 54–67.

atic. He should exhaustively enumerate the distinctively different courses of action open to the opponent as a response to each of his own possible moves, and in light of these settle on his own best course of action. Further, Harry may find it desirable to work out a strategy, that is, a framework of different courses of action, each linked in advance to a possible choice of the opponent, such that howsoever the opponent acts, Harry automatically will have a considered move with which to reply immediately. For example, in the case of the lion, Harry can decide to play thusly: as long as the lion seems not to see him, freeze, but the moment the lion does seem to spot him, make for the tree. Contingent decisions can introduce time to the game, with one player having to wait until the other player makes his move—what in the literature is called an "extensive," not a "normative" game.

By the term *position* I shall refer to the place Harry has arrived at in his game against the other. Harry's position is created by the past opportunities he did and did not avail himself of, and consists in the framework of possible moves (with their probability of success) that are now open to him.

Given an extensive game, one can characterize intermediate moves (and the positions they give rise to) in various ways, an important instance being the distinction between *viable* and *nonviable* ones, where the concern is whether or not a particular move, however much the player sacrifices by making it, still leaves him able to continue on with the game should his move prove unsuccessful.[23] Similarly, one can speak of viable and nonviable positions.

Now it is possible to review the defining conditions for *strategic interaction*.[24] Two or more parties must find themselves in a well-structured situation of mutual impingement where each party must make a move and where every possi-

---

[23] This issue is developed at length in K. Boulding, *Conflict and Defense* (New York: Harper Torchbooks, 1963), ch. 4, "The Theory of Viability," pp. 58–79.

[24] The label is mine; the notion that there may here be an intelligible area in its own right I take from T. C. Schelling.

ble move carries fateful implications for all of the parties. In this situation, each player must influence his own decision by his knowing that the other players are likely to try to dope out his decision in advance, and may even appreciate that he knows this is likely. Courses of action or moves will then be made in the light of one's thoughts about the others' thoughts about oneself. An exchange of moves made on the basis of this kind of orientation to self and others can be called strategic interaction. One part of strategic interaction consists of concrete courses of action taken in the real world that constrains the parties; the other part, which has no more intrinsic relation to communication than the first, consists of a special kind of decision-making—decisions made by directly orienting oneself to the other parties and giving weight to their situation as they would seem to see it, including their giving weight to one's own. The special possibilities that result from this mutually assessed mutual assessment, as these effect the fate of the parties, provide reason and grounds for employing the special perspective of strategic interaction.

Once it is seen that the players' situation in regard to mutual assessment is crucial, one can see that games will be possible where opposition does not exist. For there will be situations where two parties find it in their individual interests to coordinate their courses of action, but must do this while restrictions are known to prevail on what each player knows and can learn about the plans of the other. Harry and his other need not be opponents; they can be fellow-conspirators. For this reason the use of the term "opponent" for Harry's co-participant is a little loose if not wrong. Nonetheless, in the typical case, Harry and the other are locked in conflict such that any gain for one is exactly balanced by a loss to the other —the so-called zero-sum game. And here the main ideas of game theory can be placed: the notion of saddle point as a "solution" to the game; the notion of "mixed strategies" as a means of transforming all two-person zero-sum games into ones for which a solution is possible; the use of the concepts of coalition and dominance as a means of dealing with games involving more than two parties and three or more choices.

III

The gamey situations which have been considered so far are tight and pure. Once nature, self-interest, and an intelligent opponent are assumed, nothing else need be; strategic interaction follows. And, in fact, some of the developments in game theory require no more than these minimal assumptions, the object being to find a desirable strategy for Harry in the face of opponents as intelligent and amoral as himself.

One of these developments in the analysis of pure games is important for us here. It has to do with the role of assessability, especially as this pertains to communication. The problem here is what has come to be called "credibility."

Earlier I suggested that the player, Harry, is concerned to assess his situation and if another player is part of this situation, this other will be looked to in forming the assessment. We can think of this second player, the other or opponent, as contributing in two ways to this assessment. First, he can *give off expressions* which, when gleaned by Harry, allow the latter to make some sense out of what is happening and to predict somewhat what will happen. (In this the opponent presumably is no better than lesser animals and even inanimate objects, all of which can serve as a source of information.) Second, the opponent can *transmit communications*, that is, convey linguistic avowals (or substitutes thereof). These Harry can (and is openly meant to) receive, and is meant to be informed thereby. Some special attention should be given to communications in the analysis of strategic interaction, for many games involve this kind of activity.

Certain statements made to Harry by his opponent can have crucial relevance for whatever is gamey in the situation between them. Harry's opponent can make an *unconditional avowal* regarding his intention to follow a stated course of action, affirming that regardless of what Harry does, he is going to do so and so. More important still, the opponent can make a *conditional avowal*, claiming that he will pursue a given course of action if Harry does (or does not) engage in another given course of action. Two basic possibilities are involved here. There is the *promise*, where the outcome conditionally proposed is something Harry can be assumed to desire, and there is the *threat*, where the conditionally proposed outcome is something Harry would presumably like to avoid.[25]

All avowals can be described in terms of their correctness, that is, whether or not what they state accords with the facts. And they can be described according to whether they are believed or not by their maker. Avowals also raise the issue of resolve: that is, does the maker have the temperamental inclination to make every possible effort to carry out his intention? And finally, there is the issue of capability: given a high resolve, does the actor have the resources at his command to execute his design?

Given these independent factors relevant to the significance of avowals, we can begin to see some of the confusions possible in a term like "credibility." When an avowal is made to Harry, he can be concerned about its correctness, the other's belief and resolve in making it, or capability in regard to carrying it out, or—and most likely of all—some unanalyzed combination of these factors. Credibility itself is not to be confused with a more specific phenomenon, trustworthiness, namely, the warrantability of trust, defining trust as the reli-

---

[25] Promises and threats can be defined as passing responsibility for an outcome on to the recipient and as connecting the reputation of the maker to carrying out something that is otherwise against his interests. Students of strategy can then distinguish promises and threats from encouragements and warnings, the latter two terms referring to predictions made to Harry concerning the incidental effects of his pursuing a particular course of action. See Schelling, *op. cit.*, pp. 123ff. and F. Iklé, *How Nations Negotiate* (New York: Harper & Row, 1964), pp. 62ff.

ance Harry gives through his own actions to classes of the other's avowals based on consideration of the latter's "moral character." [26]

The willingness of an individual to credit another's unconditional and conditional avowals is an entirely necessary thing for the maintenance of collaborative social activity and, as such, a central and constant feature of social life. Nonetheless, this does not tell us why (and where) individuals show this reliance when, in fact, they do.

The issue of self-belief alone (as one ingredient in credibility) presents crucial problems. Surely it is in the nature of words that it will always be physically possible to employ them unbelievingly. And there will always be situations when it will be in the other's interests to lie to Harry. Given these facts of life, will it not be wise for Harry always to suspect the other of misrepresentation, and for the latter to suspect that he will thus be suspected, whether innocent or not? The native spearsmen game provides an example: Harry's opponent, should he speak the language, can say, "Put aside your spear, Harry, and let us discuss a method of getting out of the predicament we find ourselves in, for surely the chance each of us has of getting the other is not worth the cost of failing to do so." But how could Harry possibly know but that as soon as he lowers his spear, the speaker will have at him? Why should Harry accept verbal promises, and why should he who promises bind himself by the ones he makes?

A common language, then, may be a necessary condition for credible communication, but is certainly not a sufficient one. Following Schelling, a quite fundamental question must be put: how does it, and why should it, come to pass that any weight at all is ever given to words; what is it that makes avowals credible? To repeat: Since the other's interests will

---

[26] The leading experiments here are those of Morton Deutsch. See his "Trust and Suspicion," *Conflict Resolution*, 2 (1958), 265–279, and "Cooperation and Trust: Some Theoretical Notes," *Nebraska Symposium on Motivation*, 1962, pp. 275–320.

often be served by his making threats and promises, it seems reasonable to assume that his interests will also be frequently served by his making false or empty, that is, self-disbelieved, threats and promises. But it is also reasonable to assume that Harry will appreciate that it is in the other's interests to bluff, and therefore it is wise to discount his statements and not take them at face value. The other in turn, appreciating this view of his avowals that Harry is wise to have, will find himself in a fundamental predicament: whether he believes in his own avowal or not, how can he convince Harry to do so? In short, since words can be faked, what grounds can self-respecting players have for putting faith in any of them?

To proceed now it will be convenient to complicate our original approach to Harry. Until now we have set Harry up as the one making an assessment, leading, finally, to his assessment of the other's expressions and communications. But of course, in his dealings with the other, Harry will be giving off expressions and transmitting communications also. And just as this information will be crucial to the other, so, by virtue of the interdependency of their situation, will it be crucial to him who provides it, namely Harry. Thus, just as Harry will be concerned about the credibility of the other's avowals, so will he be concerned about the credibility of his own. For purposes of analysis, Harry and his other now become interchangeable. Harry becomes not merely someone making an assessment, but also someone providing the basis for assessment.

It might seem that a scenario could easily be constructed in which two parties would come to see that the payoff they were to receive was to be an equal sharing of anything they could earn separately or together.[27] In these circumstances each player would have a continuing reason for giving weight to the communications of the other, since it is only in this

---

[27] As distinguished from the "prisoner's dilemma" game, where an equally divided payoff is only one of the possibilities, and where mutual trust is not situationally generated.

way that a maximum coordination of activity is possible, and hence a maximally effective effort. Under this arrangement of self-interest, mutual credence would be situationally facilitated during the course of the interaction, apart from the opinion either of the two parties might have about the trustworthiness of the other. The two parties would presumably act as two players on the same team. Face value would be accorded words, even in the absence of any normative grounds for doing so. The correctness of statements might be challenged, but not their sincerity.

However, circumstances under which mutual communication credence could arise in this nonnormative way seem to be quite limited. Often the collaborative activity may make for mutual credence, but the moment the game is over, or even approaches its termination, it may pay one player to try to rob the other of his share, or to worry about being robbed and consequently take protective measures—as illustrated in such stories as *The Treasure of Sierra Madre*. Further, although two players can come to see that their interests are joint, each may not be in a position to convey to the other that this has been seen, and even when they can, each may have no way of demonstrating that his own avowal that their interests are joint is self-believed; for this is just the sort of avowal that would be made by someone who was trying to trick others into crediting him.

One must return, then, to circumstances where each player is not ready to assume that he can do best by working trustfully with the other and ask how each, under these circumstances, can find reasonable grounds for relying on the other's words.

First, to clear the ground, one ought to consider the weight that can be given to something that looks like words, but actually does not function like them. For although the prototype of a strategic course of action consists of a gross alteration in the physical circumstances of the party, under certain special conditions, the conveying of a programmed signal will suffice. Return to Harry the pilot. Just as it is thinkable for his parachute to be activated by a lever in the cockpit, so it is thinkable for it to be activated by a programmed speech sound. Our pilot could then execute his move, committing himself to a course of action by means of what looks like a verbal statement. But of course, what one has here is an environment engineered with malice aforethought to give objective force to simulated statements, and Harry, in giving a verbal signal, is doing no more or less than he could do were he to parachute by crawling out of the plane and pulling a ripcord. The fable of Ali Baba and the Forty Thieves carries this arrangement one step further: the oral signal "Open Sesame" serves to open a mountain door by virtue of a concealed work force chained to a winch and disciplined to respond on cue. Again, however, we merely have a simulation of communication because the words employed are tied to a specified outcome by impersonal rigid means, instead of drawing their meaning from the general rules of the language as supported by a linguistic community.

There is a second marginal possibility which seems surely to involve communication but in a very special way does not. Harry and his opponent can come together in a face-to-face social encounter and engage in what might be called banter or verbal jousting. The resources to be drawn upon are all the wittily insulting things that each player can say about the other, while at the same time denying the other an opening from which to top the efforts that have been made against him, or to survive them with equanimity. The players are then faced with a dilemma, and hence a game: nothing ventured, nothing gained, and yet, the bigger the venture, the more is lost if the sally should lack suitability and grace or be returned in kind without flustering the recipient. Now the interesting thing about this kind of jousting is that statements don't have to be self-believed or correct, and they don't have to be binding; they just have to be imaginative and apt, providing, of course (and it is here that norms begin to enter), that they are within the realm of bantering decorum. These statements, unlike most, have a consummatory status, not a promissory one; they are moves, in the manner of a belt in the chin.

A related possibility is found in those games where self-unbelieved statements are a permitted part of play. In poker, for example, bluffing is allowed not only by making misleading bets, and by conveying misleading gestural expression, but also through words. The price of providing incorrect verbal statements is the chance that opponents will learn more about one's actual hand from these misdirections than they would from scrupulously decorous play. When Harry's opponent purportedly expresses and communicates his feelings about his hand, he is, in effect, challenging Harry to a duel, the implied claim being that he is better at concealing than Harry is at uncovering. At the next deal, Harry can reverse roles and try his hand at bluffing the opponent. Casino 21 offers a less-developed example of the same opportunity. When the dealer has a 10-count card "up" he is obliged to check his hole card against the possibility of a blackjack. Experienced players sometimes try to "read" the dealer's expression at this juncture in order to determine whether or not he has a "stiff." Dealers suspect that they must be giving something away by their expression, and partly in response to this, they sometimes try to provide false cues. A tacit contest regarding expression results.

The three cases I have mentioned, oral signal engineering, verbal jousting, and bluff games, share one crucial feature: words are employed effectively without the question arising as to why the parties should put stock in them. The matter of trust cannot be at issue. Other situations can be cited which appear, at least at first, to avoid the same difficulty.

In the auction business a very minor signal is often taken as a committed bid. Of course, in some auctions a deposit is required before the individual can make a bid, this constituting an instance of "earnest" money. In many other cases, however, no such control is employed. Now it appears that the feasibility of honoring gestures derives from the fact that before the bid-won article is taken from the auction room, it must be paid for. In effect, then, what has been bid for is not the article, but the right to claim it at a particular price. And what is being offered up trustingly by the House is not the article but the opportunity of selling it on that particular occasion. A mere signal *is* being taken seriously, but not as seriously as one might at first imagine. A similar situation prevails in the brokerage business. It takes very little demonstration of financial competence (although there are rulings obliging brokers to know their customers) to induce a broker to make a large purchase on the basis of a telephone order from the presumed buyer. Here, if anywhere, mere words are taken quite seriously. However, since the firm does not give up legal possession of the purchased stock until payment is received, and since by law payment must be received within five days, all that the firm actually risks in taking a customer on faith is the price-differential of the stock between the time of purchase and the time payment is due.[28]

In the case both of auctions and brokerage sales, it is easy to feel that the words of the customer must be trusted and to seek in such factors as "concern for one's reputation" for the grounds of trust. Perhaps faith in the efficacy of such normative elements is important in speeding up transactions and easing the mind of the seller. But this should not blind us to the presence of arrangements of an entirely extramoral kind which, in fact, underlie the practicality of these trusting relations.

The examples of auctions and brokerage ordering can be seen as special cases of a more general possibility. Verbal communication in the absence of a normative basis for trust

---

[28] It should be said that there have been occasions when this price differential, purposely created and purposely exploited, has cost a victimized brokerage firm considerable, but hardly enough to threaten solvency. A case report may be found in *The Wall Street Journal*, February 1, 1961, p. 18, "SEC Charges 3 Men Manipulated Prices of Polaroid, IBM Stock through Fraud."

ought to be possible whenever the speaker can show the listener that there is relatively little to lose in crediting his words—a reduction of the need for trust by a reduction of what is entrusted.

Some further examples of untrusting credibility may be cited. If the other uses words to draw Harry's attention to objective nonverbal evidence as to the correctness of the assertions, then these words ought to be effective regardless of how little Harry may trust mere words; after all, he is only gambling the direction of his attention and may lose very little, should the attended evidence prove unconvincing. (This is not the case, of course, in the famous "Watch out behind you," trap.) Similarly, the other, under pressure to divulge where he has hidden money, or evidence, or anything else that he admits to having hidden, can provide the demanded information, knowing that, and knowing that Harry knows that, the absolute proof of the good faith and correctness of his statements will soon be evident. Providing Harry retains control over the speaker until the information is checked out, Harry may find that the cost of taking the other at his word is only the cost of following directions. The latter can then feel that even though Harry has every reason to mistrust him, Harry will still find it useful to extend trust temporarily in this regard. Of course, should the speaker *really* not know where the stuff is hidden, and says so, he will find himself in the awkward position of having to take the same position that he would take, were he trying to conceal information that he actually had. Note that information that can't be proved out in some way should hardly be worth the effort to obtain, for what grounds can be created for trusting what is received?

One more illustration. A joint plan of action verbally proposed by an untrustworthy opponent might be safely given weight by Harry if the plan proposes a sequence of steps simultaneously or alternatively taken by both, such that no *one* step appreciably jeopardizes its taker's position. Thus, our two hostile spearsmen could, following the verbal suggestion of one of them, lower their spears together, leave them on the ground, and both move away, in opposite directions along the circle of the clearing until each described a half-circle and found himself at the other's spear, but now next his own land, not the enemy's—and all this without giving the other enough advantage at any point to render acceptance of the scheme dangerous.[29]

As a final comment on the issue of credibility in statements, the law might be considered, for here the issue of belief is the center of much conscious concern. Accusations that Harry makes against himself tend to be given more weight than those he makes against others, presumably on the assumption that the less an individual has to gain by a statement the more it can be credited. In any case, should Harry make an accusation against himself, it will be credited sufficiently to call forth an investigation—unless there are obvious counterindications having to do with age, sobriety, or sanity—but if no corroborating facts appear, no *corpus delicti*, then the con-

---

[29] See Schelling, *op. cit.*, p. 95. Other "good" reasons for giving weight to mere words can be found. Daniel Elsberg suggests some:

Let me just say what I think the impact of words on expectations is. Words can suggest hypotheses which might not have occurred to the person otherwise, or focus attention on these hypotheses, which can then be tested much more precisely. Specifically, in the Prisoner's Dilemma game, if I plan to punish the person not once but three times, I want him to test that hypothesis, and I want his expectations to go in that direction. Without words, that n. ght be very hard to do. He defects once. I defect. He thinks, "Well, maybe he's just punishing me once. I'll cooperate again." I defect again, and then again. He thinks, "What the hell is going on? He's crazy." So he defects, and now I have to defect three more times. The message can get very cloudy. If, however, I told him, "You watch. Defect once, and I defect three times. Three times and that's it," it gives him something to watch. He tests it, and he finds out. It affects his expectations much more precisely than rather ambiguous actions do. [In K. Archibald, *Strategic Interaction and Conflict* (Institute of International Studies, 1966), p. 218]

A useful treatment of the basis for giving weight to mere words in international relations is R. Jervis, *The Logic of Images in International Relations* (Princeton: Princeton University Press, 1970), ch. 4, "Signals and Bluffs."

fessor will not be charged. Further, when Harry's presumed statements aren't made by him directly to official ears but rather relayed thereto by another, then the latter's reportings tend to be defined as mere "hearsay." Exceptions are made and credence is given to relayed statements when (as already suggested) these run counter to the interests of the relayer, or when he can claim the statements represent Harry's dying declarations, or that the statements are *res gestae*, namely, heard from Harry's lips during the heat of the moment upon which the statements bear.[30]

It is possible, then, to point to situations where mere words appear to be given weight, but upon examination it turns out that not much weight is actually given to them in these cases. How, then, does it become possible for mere avowals to play a role in strategic interaction?

A gamey answer is the concept of "commitment," as developed by Schelling. He who avows (or expresses) a contingent course of action can back up his stand by arranging to remove himself from the physical circumstances that would allow him to alter his indicated course of action, or by arranging to give up control of the schedule of payoffs that make anything but adherence to his indicated plan very costly.

Perhaps the best known of such devices is "deposit" or "earnest" money;[31] hostaging of self or loved ones is another.

---

[30] See, for example, J. Fisher, *The Art of Detection* (Sterling Paperbacks, 1961), p. 108.

[31] If a prospective buyer makes a bid on a house put up for sale, the seller finds himself in double jeopardy. If he agrees to the sale and withdraws his house from the market, the bidder can decide he prefers to rent an apartment and invest his capital in securities. The owner can then find that he has foregone possible sales at a time when the market may have been temporarily good. Earnest money, which the bidder gives over physically to the escrow company, can, in theory, be calculated to exactly compensate for the money worth of foregone selling opportunities. It is then a matter of financial indifference to the owner whether or not the bidder goes through with his offer. Verbal protestations of intent to buy have ceased then to be anything that the seller need give weight to. The second contingency from which earnest money protects the seller is vulnerability to haggling. When the

Still another means of commitment is to expend resources on the initial phases of a course of action such that the continuation of the plan becomes mandatory, and then to expose direct evidence of the expenditure to the enemy. (But of course, this device can only be used for unconditional avowals, not conditioned ones.) Note that in all these cases, words themselves are not what give weight to promises or threats; what gives credit to avowals is the objective appearance of persuasive evidence that a proposed course of action has been unretractably entered upon or linked to payoffs which overwhelmingly motivate it. If the player cannot arrange for this evidence, then in many cases no game-relevant interaction will be possible between the parties, or least ought not to be.

IV

Although the issue of commitment is of central importance in the analysis of game strategies, the empirical study of strategic interaction must proceed beyond this point. The idea of all-out, "zero-sum," opposition, and of a pure and tight game, does not cover all that is to be considered. And while the notion of a game of coordination expands matters a little, too much is still left out. For in real-life situations it is usually the case that gamelike interactions occur in a context of constraining and enabling social norms. For game theory as such, these norms can be usefully treated as a regrettable limitation on the game-worthiness of players—a matter to be temporarily set aside so that analysis can proceed. Or norms can be treated as conditions of the game, or something whose maintenance is defined as an interest of the parties. For the sociologist, however, these normative limita-

---

seller agrees to accept a bid, he exposes himself to the bidder's withdrawal of the original offer on some excuse and the replacement of the bid with a slightly lower one—which, in turn, can be reduced if it is accepted. Thus, it is possible to peg earnest money so as to make it uneconomical for the bidder to haggle.

tions on pure gaming—limitations which ideal games themselves help to point out—may be the matter of chief interest. Let us proceed, then, to bring our little scenarios closer to life in various ways. It will be found that Harry and his opponent still need to be able to commit themselves to avowals, but that now they are in a much better position to do so.

One can begin by noting that Harry's situation with fire, plane, lion, or other can be seen in terms of the constraints, restrictions, and controls that dominate his activity. These must be analytically differentiated.

First, there is the *constraint to play*. Once in these gamey situations, Harry cannot decide to disdain the play or postpone it; his doing nothing itself becomes, in effect, a choice and a course of action. Second, there are constraints regarding courses of action. Harry is not faced with a vast choice of moves, each a little different from the others, or with the possibility of creating variations and modifications; he is faced with a finite and often quite limited set of possibilities, each of which is clearly different from the others. Harry's situation, in other words, is *structured*.[32] Third, once he decides on a given move and initiates it, he cannot change his mind; he becomes *committed* to it. Fourth, a tight connection exists between the game and the payoff. In the illustrations given earlier, life and death are involved, however much Harry might wish he were playing for less serious stakes. More important, the courses of action taken and the administration of losses and gains in consequence of play are part of the same seamless situation, much as is in duels of honor, where the success of the swordsman's lunge and the administration of an injury are part of a single whole. I shall speak here of an *intrinsic payoff*.

The four factors here described—constraint to play, structuring of choices, commitment to moves made, intrinsic

---

[32] As already suggested, this may be of a more practical than theoretic constraint.

114

payoff—taken together are sometimes referred to as an *enforcement system.*

In the scenarios already cited, enforcement is largely ensured by the natural world in conjunction with Harry's unalterable human equipment. And we deal with tight little games; there is nothing much that Harry can do to modify the terms on which he is constrained to act. Even in his opposition to other the spearsman, this is the case: given the mutual animosity of the tribes, the layout of the territories, and the nature of spears and of the arms that throw them, Harry's predicament is inevitable and inescapable. (And in fact, thinkable solutions, such as a step-by-step, simultaneous movement by both players to their own sides, are not likely to loosen matters, since suspicious gamesmen are not likely to trust schemes suggested by the enemy no matter how safe and mutually advantageous they seem.)

An important step in loosening up the game is made when enforcement power is taken from mother nature and invested in a social office specialized for this purpose, namely, a body of officials empowered to make final judgments and to institute payments. Once this is done, a crucial wedge is driven between courses of action and outcome. Since the judges and their actions will not themselves be fully fixed in the natural environment, many unnatural things are possible.

First off, and most important, in cases where the payment for a player's move ceases to be automatic but is decided on and made by the judges after everything is over, the move itself becomes subtly reduced in status; the move, in fact, becomes a mere device for making points in a recreational type of game. When Harry, the gladiator, is obliged to hold up delivering the *coup de grâce* to his fallen opponent so that some designated portion of the audience can decide whether death or mercy is to be administered, Harry has had his fight transformed into a contest—one that could equally well be carried out over a Ping-Pong table. Similarly with a sword duel. In the modern version of wired players and electrical foils, the successful lunge ceases to be an intrinsic part of the injury that is administered and becomes merely a means of racking up the flashing lights of a score. And this point score can be paid in the form of reprieve from a death penalty that was to have been exacted at another time and place, or the hand of the fair princess in marriage, or a silver trophy cup, or green stamps.[33]

What has been described is an arrangement by which the scoring system and the awarding of payoffs are physically separated and only arbitrarily and *extrinsically* linked, and this latter by a socially organized system of sanctions. In these circumstances the way becomes clear to admitting all kinds of verbal signals and codified gestures as effective moves. As will be considered later, the judges need only "recognize" such signals as binding on their makers, and the players will find that mere words aren't mere any more but have full weight.

Now we must see that when the game is socially mediated, when it is "loose," a new set of important possibilities occur.

First, there are "frame" issues: Does the player mean his move to be taken seriously, taken as a real move, or is he merely kidding, toying or fumbling with the tokens, rehearsing, and so forth?

Associated with the question of frame there is the issue of misperception. A clear hit in mortal swordplay can perfectly well occur in a foggy night, the clarity of the hit having to do with its physiological consequences for the hit organism. But in games where hits are merely points, a move must often be terminated with an act of perceptual clarity, lest there be a dispute as to what, in fact, has actually happened. A signifi-

---

[33] In fact, in England there was the institution of trial by champion in which the principals, with ropes around their necks, awaited fatefully the outcome of a duel fought by proxy specialists—in short, duels to someone else's death. See R. Baldick, *The Duel* (London: Chapman & Hall, 1965), p. 14.

cant part of the training of casino dealers, for example, turns upon that issue. The aim is to ensure that the designative features of the environment of play remain absolutely clear and stable so that no argument can possibly arise as to what, in fact, has taken place.

Another new possibility found in loose games is cheating, a process that highlights the difference between automatic natural enforcement agencies with intrinsic payoffs and social enforcement agencies employing extrinsic payoffs. It is apparent that where enforcement is part of implacable nature, cheating is not possible—it is not even thinkable. But where judges have to attend to points, trickery of various kinds will always be possible.

Closely related to cheating is a further possibility, that of bribery and influence. Judges, being human, can always be got to. For example, Harry, a student pilot, in being examined for his license, may be given a simulated crisis in a stationary training plane, his electrically recorded activity with dead controls taken as a test score. Here it is not nature or a socially created environment which steps in to enforce the payoff but a duly authorized examining board using mere scores as the basis of judgment. Now, for many candidates, an examining board may seem to be quite like nature, something that can't be tampered with, asked for mercy, or effectively anticipated. But in fact, examining boards can be appealed to, got round, infiltrated, subverted, and even coerced or intimidated into changing a decision; in addition, their test can be doped out in advance and even leaked.

Also, in most decisions handed down by judges, enforcement of payoff does not rest on sheer coercion, as it does when nature calls the tune in matters of life and death. Other factors are involved: the sentiment that judges are sacred and their word should not be openly challenged; the capacity of judges to inflict extra penalties of a steeper kind should their judgment be rejected, and still steeper penalties should this, in turn, be rejected, and so forth, eventually culminating pre-

117

sumably in physically coerced rulings. In many cases, then, the loser of a game is in a position to decline, temporarily at least, to accept cooperatively the judgment against him, and it may be well worth his while to do so.[34]

There will be many games, in consequence, that have a second tacit little game attached to the end of them. Harry must ask himself: "Is it worth my while or not to undertake the cost and risk of bypassing, subverting, or challenging the enforcement system?"

A final point about loose games. In game situations where nature or human engineering ensures that enforcement will be implacable and automatic, one is likely to find that such courses of action as are open to Harry are completely open to him: he has within himself and under his own control all the capacities that are needed in order to initiate and execute the move he chooses. However, when a social agency is the force behind the enforcement system and a separation is made between the scoring and the payoff, then the role of the player as an effective agent changes. The physical capacity to make the move may entirely cease to be an issue, since in many socially enforced games the move itself is merely a token one—the pushing of a counter from one square to another, for example. However, a new issue becomes prominent: whether or not the player is authorized to commit his party, that is, play for it, and if so, what limits are placed upon what he can do in its name.[35]

---

[34] The principal exception is the death penalty, the only practical means of refusing to play the game after all appeals have been tried is to take one's own life first.

[35] Here we have the nice issues dealt with in the law of agency. The British version can be found in G. Chesire and C. Fifoot, *The Law of Contract* (London: Butterworths, 1964), ch. 2, "Privity of Contract under the Law of Agency," pp. 400–432. Note that the player is not the only one who can cause difficulty. In Europe up to 1919 the actions of an authorized representative in international negotiations tended to bind his government; since then—with the U.S.A. leading the way because of the need and vagaries of Senate ratification—nation parties have considerably weakened the power of their players to make commitments. Here see Nicolson, *op. cit.,* pp. 44–46.

I have argued that games which rely on a social enforcement system become exposed to many issues which tight games are free of. Nonetheless, it might still be claimed that the limitations of the gaming model herein reviewed are manageable ones. There are, however, other limitations of a general kind that are less so.[36] Persons often feel that agencies, especially nations, can be defined as conditions of adjustive action, not opponents in a game. Further, persons often don't know what game they are in or whom they are playing for until they have already played. Even when they know about their own position, they may be unclear as to whom, if anybody, they are playing against, and, if anyone, what his game is, let alone his framework of possible moves. Knowing their own possible moves, they may be quite unable to make any estimate of the likelihood of the various outcomes or the value to be placed on each of them. And bad moves often lead not to clear-cut penalties conceptualized as such but rather to diffuse and straggling undesired consequences— consequences which result when persons do something that throws them out of gear with the social system. Of course, these various difficulties can be dealt with by approximating the possible outcomes along with the value and likelihood of each, and casting the result into a game matrix; but while this is justified as an exercise, the approximations may have (and be felt to have) woefully little relation to the facts.

V

Review the development along which we have taken Harry. On one side there is a party and an authorized player who commits the party to a hopefully best course of action in a situation made up of the possible courses of action open to it and to the opponent. On the other side there is nature (pure or socially impregnated), or a social agency, either of which has the job of enforcing play, structuring

---

[36] Here and elsewhere I am grateful to Amélie Rorty for suggestions.

choices, committing the party to the player's move, and enforcing a particular payoff. *Interaction*, then, from Harry's point of view, refers to the following sequence: assessment, decision-making, initiating a course of action, and payoff. Where a social agency is involved as enforcer, moves can be made by means of a communication, but communication, at least in the narrow sense of that term, is not analytically relevant or necessary.

We can illustrate where we have gone, and go on from there, by looking at "equipment games" such as checkers, bridge, craps, and the like.

All equipment games provide means by which intrinsic game resources can be allocated to the parties at play, and their players allowed to commit these resources to a prediction whose correctness or incorrectness is then determined by the equipment in play functioning as a decision machine. The coming together of the participants into play activates the game equipment, including its resources, plays, and outcome decisions.

In a game such as casino craps, the several functions of the game equipment are kept relatively separate. The "layout" provides a clear depiction of the full array of played-for outcomes—the matrix of possible moves. The dice provide a decision machine for determining which of the possible outcomes actually come out. The chips alone have a multiple function. They constitute the extrinsic resources for the payoff; [37] they serve as tokens for announcing and displaying a player's decision; they function as pawns, namely resources the player lets out of his control, thus committing himself to

---

[37] It is easy to confuse the issue here. Checkers and chess pieces are part of the internal resources of their respective games; they are therefore limited in number and value by the rules of the game and can be translated into extrinsic values only when seen as part of the overall game result, which result is accorded a particular extrinsic value such as money, silver cups, or kudos. Gambling chips are not part of any particular game, but rather part of the casino bank's substitute currency, transferable on demand into ordinary currency, much like ordinary currency, on a grander scale, is sometimes transferable into silver or gold, on demand made to the State.

a particular self-predicted outcome. Note that a special kind of committing of resources—a special kind of move—is involved, the kind that necessarily conveys to all concerned the predicted outcome to which the player has committed his resources. The situation here is like that of Harry and the lion, except that crap shooting arrangements are quite intentionally designed so as to ensure that all moves are visible.

In games such as checkers, game functions are less segregated than in craps. In checkers (as in craps), the board depicts the set of possible moves. The checkers constitute the intrinsic resources of the game as well as pawns, namely the means for openly establishing the player's alignment of committed forces. The decision device is also found in the positioned checkers, namely a special configuration of two opposing checkers in combination with a "capturing" rule. In card games such as bridge, the game equipment has an even heavier overlay of multiple functions. The layout is cut up into 52 pieces and distributed evenly among the players, who also use these pieces as intrinsic resources. As in checkers, the win-lose decisions are generated by a specified juxtaposition of the committed resources of opponents in conjunction with a "taking" rule.

All equipment games can be, and some usually are, complicated by linking the game-relevant intrinsic resources to extrinsic ones, usually, but not necessarily, money. The linkage, of course, can be in terms of any arbitrarily selected scale of equivalents. In games such as poker and craps, money can (but need not) be directly put in pawn, thus making the translation from game resources to extrinsic ones unnecessary.

Now the central question can be put: what system of enforcement is employed to ensure that the game will be played in the right "spirit," that is, that once the player makes a move, he will abide by his action and not, for example, change his mind in mid-play or withdraw his bet or refuse to let go of it, or claim he is not "really" playing, or tip the table over?

First, take games played in legitimate casinos, games involving a party pitted against a well-banked social establishment that plays and pays in a programmed fashion. What enforcements are present? [38]

The payoff is money, the value of which the party is assumed to accept. The casino runs a side business of bilaterally exchanging chips for money or for bank checks from customers on demand; it also gives and receives bets in this local currency, and the player must accept this temporary substitute. Although casinos have gone bankrupt, rendering their chips worthless, this is not common, so that ordinarily the cashable value of the chips is assured. This means that while chips are in a sense "merely" symbols, they certainly aren't merely symbols as roses or flags can be merely symbols; ordinarily a chip represents a very clear-cut exactable claim, much as money is a claim.

Adherence to rules of the game is enforced by casino guards and, behind them, the city or county police. In point of fact, however, these agencies need rarely be called on in this capacity. Casinos are constantly plagued and have been destroyed by cheating on the part of customers and employees. Casinos have even had to deal with counterfeit chips. But no casino complains of players declining to let go of a lost bet. The actions and even the mere presence of guards and police do not seem necessary here. For the relevant basis of enforcement, I think we must look elsewhere. In casinos the table layout is such that how much is bet, what outcome the bet is committed to, and what the outcome actually is, are all crystal clear and easily witnessed. The layouts of the various games also ensure that the player will have physically let go of, and ecologically separated himself from, the money or chips he bets. At the same time, dealer behavior is designed to affirm that bets have denominational, not monetary, value —mere counters differing from one another only in terms of the number of counters the casino must match up against them. These arrangements, in conjunction with the institu-

---

[38] Comments on casino gambling are based on a Nevada field study in preparation.

tionalization of what might be called the "spirit of play"—and not the presence of guards—seem to provide the enforcement that makes the placement of chips a real commitment.[39]

When one turns from casino games to private self-policed ones, new enforcement issues arise. "Blanket" craps is strictly regulated: money itself is used as the pawn and there is a full accounting and transfer of funds at the end of each brief hand. But private poker is usually played with chips as a money substitute, the chips being bought at the beginning of the game (and for some players, at unfortunate times thereafter) and cashed in at the end of the evening's play. And the game is banked not by a "house" but typically by a party to the play who is recognized to be solvent and trustworthy—sometimes but not always the host. Credit is sometimes extended among the parties to the play, and collecting on these debts may be problematic (as it certainly is when extended by casinos). Beyond poker there are scores games such as gin rummy and bridge where parties must wait for the end of an evening's play before a pencil score is translated into payment by money, check, or promise.

When one turns, then, from casino games to private ones there will be looser means for translating from intrinsic resources of the games to the wider ones of the external economy. In these contexts, how can one account for the fact that players routinely act so that their placements are, in fact, commitments?

Reasons are apparent. First, there is the approved one: Harry should have incorporated the standards of sportsmanship and fair play and feel obliged to adhere to the rules of any game once he has embarked on playing it, even when he is sure he could fully conceal an infraction. Only slightly less

---

[39] Interestingly, in an environment where players very often suspect the casino of cheating them and typically exploit any easy opportunity that arises for cheating back, players, especially experienced ones, usually feel that they can mark their place at the table by leaving their chips and even cash there, knowing that howsoever dishonest the house may be, left money will be safe. Returning after a few minutes' absence, players will ordinarily not even bother to count what they return to.

approved is another reason: shame at being seen by others as someone who doesn't abide by the rules. The threat of being called a cheater or a poor sport or a disrupter of social occasions ought to be enough to bind him to the conditions of play, just as his fellow-players have been bound. And after this, there is the belief that should he acquire a reputation for welshing, he may not be able to find a future game. (It is said that among professional gamblers this latter constraint is particularly strong.)

Now it seems apparent that the less that Harry gambles of value to him outside of the game, the more likely are these normative bases of enforcement to be effective. And the more he must stake of his substance, the less likely, one might think, would he be willing to be bound by reputational considerations. Certainly there are games of a deadly kind where enemies are engaged in an all-or-nothing one-shot interaction, and where a real problem arises as to how a move can be made without a quite objective basis of commitment; for even if Harry is willing to be governed by social consideration at a time like this, he may nonetheless feel it wise to consider the possibility that his opponent will feel there is no reasonable ground for giving weight to any merely verbal promise or threat on Harry's part. After all, whatever the enforcement system, the placement of a game resource is only incidentally a communication; it is, first off, a lodgment of resources, a commitment, and where there is nothing to commit or no way of committing it, the communication can be empty indeed.

Let us now turn from equipment games, with their normatively enforced token-pawn moves, to situations where no equipment is available except the spoken word.

Earlier it was suggested that once social agencies are introduced as enforcers, it is relatively easy to support spoken statements as moves. And, in fact, there are many contexts in daily life where it is the case that if the appropriate person makes an appropriate statement, this mere talking becomes a commitment. Swearing-in rituals and wedding ceremonies are of this kind. This issue is not whether such statements

correctly reflect the facts or not, or convey self-believed sentiments or not, but that the enforcement machinery is such as
to give these verbal acts the effect of real moves. In Austin's happy phrase, these statements are "performative utter-
ances." [40] A good example is found in bridge, where the spoken word "double," as long as it is spoken in context and
"seriously," constitutes a commitment as real and unretract-
able as laying down the ace of clubs. And, of course, airlines
can even disallow joking exceptions; apparently any kind of
bomb tease in an airplane is an indictable offence.

The law, of course, provides an important instance of those
social enforcement agencies that underwrite verbal statements, and perhaps the underlying basis of all such agencies.
Under law, a whole range of verbal threats and promises become moves for which Harry can be made liable. During
court proceedings, a still wider range of verbal statements
are subject to enforcement control. The uttering of self-
disbelieved statements under oath is a punishable offence;
so also are verbal discourtesies directed at the courts. Refusal
to make a statement may itself be taken as a commitment:

> Ordinarily, when a defendant, under conditions which fairly
> afford an opportunity to reply, stands mute in the face of an
> accusation, the circumstances of his silence may be taken
> against him as evidence indicating an admission of guilt.[41]

Legal proceedings and the places where they routinely
occur are, then, places where words can have weight.[42]

---

[40] J. Austin, *Philosophical Papers,* ed. J. Urmson and G. Warnock (Oxford:
Oxford University Press, 1961), ch. 10.

[41] H. Mulbar, *Interrogation* (Springfield: Charles Thomas, 1951), p. 62.

[42] Although courts provide an environment in which words *can* have
weight, courts also ensure that words *may* be questioned. In fact, court practices provide an explicit summary of the community's conception of human
nature as it bears upon the value of a person's word even when he is under
oath:

> The credibility of a witness may be impeached on the following grounds:
> (a) by showing his general bad reputation for veracity; (b) by questioning
> him on cross-examination concerning any immoral, vicious, or criminal acts
> allegedly committed by him, which may affect his character and tend to
> show he is not worthy of belief; (c) by showing that he has been con-

There are other disciplined settings where something of the same condition prevails. In the army, the statement, "That's a command," provides a purely verbal means of pointedly invoking the full coercive power legally invested in the military. Similarly, the phrase, "Is that an order, Sir?" is a verbal means of transferring full responsibility for an act to the party requesting its performance. Both these verbal phrases constitute very real moves in the disciplined game of military discipline.

From institutional settings, where specialized ready agencies can be called upon to give weight to words, we can turn to less formal situations, situations in which the participants must themselves provide the enforcement, or where they must rely on a vague and shifting public for this service. What we find is a mosaic of ill-understood, varying practices. For example: Considerable dealings go on in business communities by means of oral agreements, especially, it might be noted, in the nonlegitimate realm, such as off-track horse-race betting. Between subordinate and superordinate in complex organizations, a verbal agreement to meet at a particular time and place is likely to firmly obligate the subordinate. It has been suggested that in Europe between the wars the heads of states gave weight to one another's words, howsoever skeptical everyone was of words coming from lower down.

What are the bases here for giving weight to words? We find a jumble of reasons notoriously difficult to disentangle from rationalizations. These have already been mentioned in connection with sportsmanship. Harry will say that he has himself to answer to, and that he would keep his word even when no one but himself could know that he had broken it. He will also say that whether or not he would like to break his word, the other has a right to be dealt with fairly, and

victed of a crime; (e) by showing that either at the time of the occurrence to which he has testified, or at the time of giving the testimony, he was under the influence of drugs or liquor or was mentally unbalanced. [Fisher *op. cit.*, p. 117]

Harry feels obliged to uphold this right. Note that there is an assumption here that a person who is a party can be a kind of moral commitment mechanism which can, within limits that are little considered, function as an enforcement machine. In fact, the popular understanding of the term "commitment" often points to such a device, implying, as it does, that the individual, within the territory of his own skin, can so discipline his will and so employ his resources as to effectively render himself his own enforcer. Harry the unmoved mover, the monad of commitment. Popular understanding adds to this the notion of emotional expression as a kind of built-in incorruptible signaling device, allowing the observer to distinguish between avowals that are to be given little weight and ones that have engaged Harry's "self-commitability." These lay beliefs, beliefs that an individual can commit himself through words and that his expression at the time will confirm his position, are fundamental, if misguided, assumptions of our strategic interactions; these beliefs run through all of our dealings with each other as if there were no other way to deal with the world, even in circumstances where suspicion is very high and the stakes are even higher. For example, during the missile crisis, Kennedy apparently was shocked that Khrushchev could give sincere-sounding assurances that no aggressive action was being planned even while missiles were being assembled in Cuba; even after discovery of this duplicity, Kennedy and his advisers still read Dobrynin's and Fomin's expressive behavior as indicative that their statements were self-believed.[43] And Kennedy was ready to con-

---

[43] In a while Robert Kennedy walked in, tired and disheveled. He had just been to see Ambassador Dobrynin in an effort to find out whether the Soviet ships had instructions to turn back if challenged on the high seas. The Soviet ambassador, the Attorney General said, seemed very shaken, out of the picture, and unaware of any instructions.

At 1:30 p.m. on Friday, John Scali, the State department correspondent for the American Broadcasting Co., received a message from Alexander Fomin, a counselor at the Soviet embassy, requesting an immediate meeting. . . . The usually phlegmatic Russian, now haggard and alarmed, said, "War seems about to break out. Something must be done." [He makes

127

duct the affairs of state in this manner even though he himself had found it expedient to have an amiable meeting with Gromyko and Dobrynin, and there play the standard game of acting as though nothing crucial was afoot when he knew that Russian missiles were in Cuba, knew that Gromyko knew this and was acting otherwise, and knew that Gromyko did not know that he knew.

One reason for giving weight to Harry's words, then, is the belief that the very design of his construction provides a window into his intent, a window to a room that is lit from within by emotional expression. In contrast, another reason to credit Harry is provided by the belief that he will abide by his word in the absence of formal enforcement because of the sheer utility of doing so. With no personal compunction against lying and no incapacity to feign expression, Harry can still feel that the chance of being discovered argues against the wisdom of the move, since once he is discovered lying, his word will no longer be given weight by anyone in any situation. Thus, it is said that the Russians are trusted to make prompt payments in connection with international trade because it is believed that they believe that a sequence of kept promises is the only way to establish a good credit rating, which is felt they feel they need. Note that the utility argument has special weight when both parties appreciate that,

---

a proposal, begs Scali to find out immediately if it is acceptable. On the same evening, after official consideration had been given to the proposal] Scali passed this word along. They met this time in the coffee shop of the Statler Hilton. Fomin, after a brief attempt to introduce the idea of U.N. inspection of Florida as well as Cuba, rose and, in his haste to get word back, tossed down a $5 bill for a $.30 check and sped off without waiting for his change. [A hopeful letter comes in two hours later from Khrushchev and everyone relaxes a little. The next morning, however, a second letter comes in from Moscow, this time with an unacceptable proposal.] Rusk called in Scali and asked him to find out anything he could from his Soviet contact. Scali, fearful that he had been used to deceive his own country, upbraided Fomin, accusing of a doublecross. The Russian said miserably that there must have been a cable delay, that the embassy was waiting word from Khrushchev at any moment. Scali brought this report immediately to the President . . . [A. Schlesinger, Jr., "A Thousand Days, Part 5," *Life*, Nov. 12, 1965]

come what may, they are destined to be required to somehow work together for many years to come. It is thus that an effort has been made to account for the fact that in some work organizations representatives of labor and of management may reserve some statements as ones to be employed with mutual appreciation that they are self-believed.[44]

However, if this pragmatic game-theoretical attitude to one's own reputation is taken, then one ought also to build up these trust credits until a time is found when the stakes are such as to make it worthwhile to expend all one's credits in a very profitable betrayal of one's word. But if Harry is advised to act in this way, then his opponent will be advised to be wary of trusting Harry in matters of the largest concern. And, as Rapaport has nicely argued,[45] if Harry anticipates this shrewdness on the opponent's part, Harry will be advised to break his word over matters of second importance, else he might not get a chance to use up his trust credits at all. But then, Harry's opponent will have a reasonable answer to this, and so on, until the basis for any trust is rationally undermined.[46]

In fact, of course, Harry and his other seldom seem to act in this way. Quite commonly, they continue to guard their own reputations and decline to cash in their credits even when they have come to the point where there would be an overall gain in doing so. Embarrassed to admit their own normative involvements, they may use the theme of enlightened long-term self-interest as a cover for their morality. But morality it is. It seems that when we are taught to make ver-

---

[44] See the useful article by P. Diesing, "Bargaining Strategy and Union Management Relationships," *Journal of Conflict Resolution*, 5 (1961), esp. 357–377. There is, of course, a natural limit to this specialization of signs: not only does it tempt misuse, but its known availability can have the consequence of reducing the credibility of avowals made without such signs. Here see Jervis, *op. cit.*, "Debasing" in ch. 4.

[45] K. Archibald, *op. cit.*, p. 98.

[46] Jervis suggests that this doleful condition of good play may be eased by the fact that in actual cases the players may not be clear as to what the other's last move is.

bal statements, we are simultaneously taught that this means telling the truth with them, especially to persons who address us while directly looking into our eyes, although of course we are also taught that there is an array of good reasons for deceiving. And when, in later years, we join in a circle of work associates or neighbors it is inevitable, it seems, that we will come to judge ourselves and others in moral terms, approving persons who are "untrustworthy," and this no matter how we actually behave or how lax we feel we can properly be in our treatment of outsiders.[47] Clearly, in the last analysis, we cannot build another into our plans unless we can rely on him to give his word and keep it, and to exude valid expressions, whether because he cannot or will not control them. It is just as clear that the virtue we demand that he have is made out of organizational necessity.

A further point should be added. Normless interaction is easy to conceive of but difficult to find or create in social nature. If Harry and his other agree to a mutually profitable exchange, it is likely, on purely physical grounds, that one will have to deliver before the other, and hence exhibit trust. Where hand-sized articles are involved, it would seem that the least presuming mode of exchange would be for Harry to let go of his offering at the very moment he takes sole hold of the other's. But even where possible, this kind of carefulness is not found. In many banks, for example, where great circumspection is usually shown in regard to many financial

---

[47] Nicolson (*op. cit.*, p. 40) provides the diplomatist's version:

As in other walks of life, and as in other professions, a man is ultimately judged, not by his brilliance, but by his rectitude. The professional diplomatist, as other men, desires deeply to be regarded as a man of honour by those whom he respects. One of the advantages of professional diplomacy under the former system was that it produced and maintained a corporate estimate of character. It was the Stock Market of diplomatic reputations. It was generally known that men such as Bülow, Aerenthal and Iswolsky were not to be wholly trusted; it was generally known that upon such men as Bethmann-Hollweg, the two Cambons, and Stolypin one could rely.

matters,[48] change is often made for a very large bill by the cashier simply taking the bill to a cash drawer at some removed point and coming back with the change, leaving the customer for a few moments with no legally foolproof evidence of having let go of anything. Here, of course, there is a tacit agreement to vest trust in the one of the two parties that might, on the face of it, seem the more trustworthy. Perhaps this division of moral labor is always to be found, at least at some point in the transaction. Thus, in skid row bottle gangs, in a milieu not noted for its businesslike dependability, a transaction may go as follows:

The initiator and the other members proceed along the sidewalk asking passers-by whether they are interested in "going in on a bottle." The solicitor has the obligation to inform the prospective partner of the amount of money collected and the number of men with whom he will have to share the wine, for example: "Three of us have 28 cents in on a bottle. Do you want to get in on it?" As the statement is made, the leader holds the announced cash out in his hand so that the prospect may know the offer is genuine and that he is not being exploited to purchase wine for a group of destitute "promoters." Thus the prospective stockholder can appraise the value of the corporation before investing.

If the solicited person has sufficient money and is willing to participate, he gives his contribution to the leader. The handing over of money toward the purchase of a "jug" of wine establishes a contractual relation by which a contributor becomes a member of the group. The contract forms a corporation in which the members hold certain rights to the consumption of the proposed bottle of wine, and the leader has the obligation to purchase and share the wine with the members. The size of the group is governed by the price of a bottle and is usually

---

[48] Banks often require, for example, that when the vault where money is stored is to be entered by a member of the staff, he be accompanied by some other member, this being a way of giving protection to the bank and getting protection from it.

131

between three and five men. The corporation continues in existence until the emptying of the bottle dissolves the contract.[49]

Here, note, trust can be minimized, but it can hardly be dispensed with completely, if on no other than organizational grounds.

Starting with Harry assessing the situation in which mother nature has placed him, we have come by stages to consider the center of communication, face-to-face informal conversation. The object is to analyze a part of what goes on in conversation by means of game-oriented concepts derived from looking at radically simplified situations. I thus assume that conversation does not provide a model to be applied elsewhere and that it is the last thing to look at, not the first.

When one attempts to characterize informal social interaction of a conversational kind, one finds that no single framework is satisfactory. As suggested, one aspect of what goes on can sometimes be analyzed as a form of banter or verbal jousting, verbal moves here having significance in spite of the absence of an enforcement system. The normative conditions that are required have to do with rules—often quite broad—of acceptable taste regarding the content of statements and with courtesies of a minimal kind obliging each player to allow the other to finish started statements. Another aspect of what goes on can be analyzed in the coldest terms: Harry can arrange to demonstrate that he has harsh penalties to invoke against those who do not take his words seriously and that there will be a bearable cost to himself should he have to do so. Also, almost always some part of face-to-face interaction can be analyzed in gamey terms by assuming that all the parties are bound by incorporated social norms regarding the absolute necessity of keeping one's word. So, too, there is the fact that in many social circles, conversations

---

[49] J. Rooney, "Group Processes among Skid Row Winos," *Quarterly Journal of Studies on Alcohol,* 22 (September 1964), 450.

among friends and acquaintances must be managed without making the kind of avowal that can be incontrovertibly shown to be self-disbelieved, unjoking, and incorrect, lest the maker seriously damage his reputation. However, in spite of these applications, the gaming approach leaves out a great deal of face-to-face conversational interaction.

During informal conversation, statements are made that are intentionally ambiguous and noncommittal. Promises and threats are made about the future under conditions where the only enforcement is the party's concern for his word, and where the other participants don't really expect or even want him to be governed by his avowals. Where others would like Harry to govern himself by a high concern for his own good reputation, Harry himself may take a more pragmatic view and show only a spotty and uncertain sensitivity regarding his own good name. He may sense that while he loses reputation in one social circle, he may remain in good repute in another, the circles themselves showing little tendency to unite for purposes of disciplining Harry. Further, parties tend in mid-play to change the payoffs they play for. Turning points are found such that what was previously merely a normative restriction on play becomes the objective of the play. (For example, the insult game can be played under the normative condition that one's social relationship to one's opponent will not be threatened. When the game is played hard, however, relationships can suddenly become threatened, and when this occurs the objective of the insulter can suddenly change. He can become someone concerned to make that verbal move which will exactly reinstate the relationship—a move that is part of a quite different game.)

There are further limitations of the gaming model. In the discussion so far, it has been assumed that Harry was to be simply a possibly sincere source of expression and a possibly honest source of statements. But this assumption is too simplifying for a realistic consideration of informal face-to-face interaction. Harry's concern to exhibit sincerity and honesty,

133

and his other's concern to be shown these qualities, can be seen in one light, as merely a reflection of something more general. It can be assumed that between any two parties in face-to-face interaction, standards of mutual respect—albeit sometimes quite minimal—will obtain. These standards apply to many aspects of behavior, of which openness is but one. In short, face-to-face interaction is an arena of *conduct*, not merely expression and communication, and conduct is judged first off not in regard to sincerity and candor, but "suitability." Certain forms of prevarication and insincerity will certainly be offensive, but also there will be many situations where a sincere expression of feelings and a candid statement of opinions will be defined as quite unnecessary if not actually offensive. Other considerations will often dominate, such as a desire and obligation to show sympathy and tact, whatever one is actually feeling.

Another point. I have argued that enforcement can be vested in a specialized agency, or the speaker himself, or, in whatever degree, the public at large. And now it is suggested that what is really enforced is not words but standards of conduct. We must go on to see that when Harry commits an offence regarding face-to-face conduct, it is often the offended party who is charged with corrective enforcement. Entirely apart from its long-range effect on Harry's reputation, mis-communication can have the effect of plunging his opponent into the business of exerting immediate negative sanctions. And here Harry's victim may not be primarily concerned with strategy or self-interest, or even with successful enforcement; his first need may be to stand up and be counted.

Of course, we can still try to apply a game perspective. When, for example, Harry makes an inappropriate statement to the other, the other is faced with a gamey dilemma. If he upholds his honor and takes umbrage, negatively sanctioning Harry in some way, then he can cause an escalation of discord; if he "lets the matter go" then he may feel that he jeopardizes his status as someone who must be taken seriously.

The clearest example of this situation is found in our popular fiction of cowboys, detectives, and other men of action. They carry guns, knives, swords, and fists as means of enforcing just treatment of themselves and such members of the gentle sex as are there to be found. Thus armed, and thus driven by personal honor, they speak words that are fateful first moves in life-and-death showdowns.[50] Note that the other's possession of enforcement equipment has a double effect; he is in a position to force Harry to keep a civil tongue, but he is also subject to exposure should he decline to bring his capabilities into play when they are called for.

A pistol and the readiness to use it—and how this can be established is a strategic problem in its own right—bring a clarity and weight to words that words don't usually have in face-to-face interaction, making cowboy fantasies almost therapeutic. Everyday interaction is certainly informed by the same chivalrous ideal, but there can be this relation between ideal and practice because it can be easily twisted in every convenient direction. Typically the offended party is neither compelled fully by honor nor governed fully by cool strategic design. He does not use his turn to make a move; he gets by with half-actions. Instead of commitments and enforcements, he provides assurances and resentments. Instead of moves, mere expressions. To translate this gestural realm entirely into strategic equivalents is to violate its regrettable nature; we end by making sustainable imputations of complex play to persons who aren't quite players and aren't quite playing.

A conclusion may be warranted. As already suggested, there could hardly be any social organization if persons could not put weight on the mere words of others; coordination of activity over time and place would become difficult indeed, and all definitions of the situation would become unstable. (Of course, a totally reliable body of persons would create special problems of its own.) Just as obviously, when mem-

---

[50] A fuller consideration is given in E. Goffman, "Where the Action Is," in *Interaction Ritual* (New York: Anchor paperback, 1967), pp. 239–277.

bers of a community are socialized into the use of speech, they are also socialized into the importance of truth telling and being reputed as truth tellers—although, of course, there are group-wide variations in this, especially in the matter of how much truth is owed to persons who can be defined as outsiders. So one is led to the common-sense view that internalized standards constitute the chief enforcement system for communication in society. But the study of these normative conditions does not so much lead to game theory as to a consideration of the varied and skittish workings of informal social control. Words are mere and shouldn't be worth anything at all, but, in fact, every statement, in one way or another, is a performative utterance.

VI

In this paper I have attempted to formulate a definition of strategic interaction and clarify the special perspective this concept implies.

It should be noted that strategic interaction is, of course, close to Meadian social psychology and to what has come to be called "symbolic interaction" [51]—since nowhere more than in game analysis does one see the actor as putting himself in the place of the other and seeing things, temporarily at least, from his point of view. Yet it is quite doubtful that there are significant historical connections between the two types of analysis. In any case, strategic interaction appears to advance the symbolic interactionist approach in two ways. First, the strategic approach, by insisting on *full* interdependence of outcomes, on mutual awareness of this fact, and on the capacity to make use of this knowledge, provides a natural means for excluding from consideration merely any kind of interdependence. This is important, for if all interdependence is

---

[51] A phrase first used in this connection by Herbert Blumer in "Social Psychology," ch. 4, in E. Schmidt, *Man and Society* (New York: Prentice-Hall, 1937), p. 153. Blumer also provides an excellent current statement in "Society as Symbolic Interaction," ch. 9, in A. Rose, *Human Behavior and Social Processes* (Boston: Houghton Mifflin, 1962), pp. 179–192.

included in the study of interaction, hardly anything distinctive can remain. Second, following the crucial work of Schelling, strategic interaction addresses itself directly to the dynamics of interdependence involving mutual awareness; it seeks out basic moves and inquires into natural stopping points in the potentially infinite cycle of two players taking into consideration their consideration of each other's consideration, and so forth.

Now the main analytical argument. The framework of strategic interaction is quite formal; no limit is placed on its application, including the type of payoff involved, as long as the participants are locked in what they perceive as mutual fatefulness and are obliged to take some one of the available, highly structured courses of action. Because of this inclusion of any kind of payoff, the game approach has an easy application to almost everything that is considered under the ill-defined rubric "interaction." Furthermore, howsoever interaction is defined, the actors involved must be accorded some attributes and given some internal structure and design, and here the propensities of a gamesman will have a place. The strategic approach will therefore always apply in some way; it is important to be clear, then, about the limits of this application.

Take the important structural realm of social relationships —their avoidance, creation, maintenance, deepening, attenuation, and termination, their linkages into networks of various kinds and functioning. Since control of the state of a relationship is a mutually interdependent objective of the persons related, strategic analysis applies. This analysis certainly adds something to our understanding of personal relating,[52] especially at certain junctures and in regard to our model of the relating entity, the individual. Nonetheless, a generalized pic-

---

[52] A thorough development may be found in P. Blau, *Exchange and Power in Social Life* (New York: Wiley, 1964). See also A. Gouldner, "Norms of Reciprocity," *American Sociological Review*, 25 (1960), 161–178; G. Homans, *Social Behavior: Its Elementary Forms* (New York: Harcourt, Brace & World, 1961); J. Thibaut and H. Kelley, *The Social Psychology of Groups* (New York: Wiley, 1959).

ture of relationship formation and the resulting structures cannot be fully delineated in strategic terms. Moreover, it appears that nothing *special* can be learned about game analysis by applying it to the field of social relationships. There *are* relationship payoffs, but these are merely instances of a larger class and play no different role in game analysis than do intrapersonal payoffs such as money-profit, "face," sexual favors, and the like—illustrated by the fact that strategic analysis of social relating typically begins with the "interests" of a single player as he balances relationship consequences off against self-possessed goods such as socioeconomic ones.[53]

From the domain of social relationships, turn to another area, to existential units of face-to-face interaction, namely, concrete gatherings such as meetings, parties, conversational circles, and the like, and to the associated rules for co-mingling. Whether to attend a social party or not, whether, once there, to allow oneself to be carried away by its spirit or not (or whether, once there, to join an available conversation cluster of low rank or remain unengaged), are decisions that can be subject to strategic analysis, as can the nature of the actor who populates these occasions. But this analysis may tell us little about the generic properties of parties (such as the rule regarding the right to join ongoing clusters and the obligation to be engaged), just as it may tell us little about the analytical structure of game theory. So, too, for example, in regard to another aspect of face-to-face interaction—greeting rules in public places. An enemy agent has a strategic problem when he is forced to decide whether to acknowledge through recognition and greeting that he is acquainted with the persons he has been brought to a prison courtyard to see get shot: [54] if it is known that he knows the victims, then failure to acknowledge the acquaintanceship can discredit his cover; if it is not known, then acknowledgment

---

[53] As described, for example, in the engaging light literature on the war between the sexes.

[54] A. Klein, *The Counterfeit Traitor* (New York: Holt, 1956), ch. 28, "The Firing Squad," pp. 172–179.

can create suspicion that could have been avoided. A husband has a similar strategic problem in joining an office secretary for a week-end flight to the Virgin Islands: if no one at the airport knows them, it may be safest to act from the beginning as the couple they will, for a time, become; if someone present knows one of them, then it may be safest for the couple to act as if they do not know each other; if someone present knows the couple's business relationship, or is likely to learn of it, then it may be safest to acknowledge that relationship with a greeting and sociable chat. (And the couple must make this decision without being able to see all the persons who will see them, and without knowing all the persons who know of them.) However, although the dilemma to recognize or not to recognize must be resolved by strategic analysis, the dilemma itself is partly produced by our rules for handling acquainted and unacquainted others during incidental public contact, and these rules are not rules of strategy but part of the mesh of norms that regulate socially organized co-mingling.

True, there are strategic moves which directly depend for their efficacy on their player being face-to-face with his opponent. Thus, an interrogator who seats his subject in a fixed chair while he sits in one that can be easily slipped along the floor can use movement to cut the subject off from a line of admission that is not useful, or to approach very close in order to evoke the natural arrangement in which his address will appear intimate, deep, and sincere. Similarly, once a subject has allowed himself to enter a state of talk, he will be constrained to reply in some way or other to questions politely asked of him, if only to complete his side of what is seen as occurring in pair sequences; given this fact, the FBI has strategic reason to conduct unpopular inquiries in person rather than by letter.[55] And yet, of course, an analysis of the *general* features of gatherings and the *general* features of

---

[55] See J. Griffiths and R. Ayres, "Faculty Note, A Postscript to the Miranda Project: Interrogation of Draft Protesters," *Yale Law Journal*, 77 (December 1967), 300–319.

strategic games turn upon different themes. Important applications of strategic interaction involve participants who are not present to each other, and sequences of moves which are not closely bound by time, whereas, generically, face-to-face gatherings entail mutual presence and brief continuities in time.

Here, surely, is a special source of confusion in the social psychological literature. The applicability of the gaming framework to relationships and gatherings, and its great value in helping to formulate a model of the actor who relates and who foregathers, has led to conceptualizations which, too quickly, intermingle matters which must be kept apart, at least initially. Social relationships and social gatherings are two separate and distinct substantive areas; strategic interaction is an analytical perspective which illuminates both but coincides with neither.

There is a third substantive area which is even easier to confuse with strategic interaction than are the two mentioned. I refer to the study of communication systems—the channels, relays, nets, transmitters, receivers, signals, codes, schedules, information loading, security checks, and other specialized practices and equipment by which, in a given organizational setting, the regular flow of explicitly formulated information is maintained.

For example, take the wireless communication system maintained between intelligence organizations and their agents in enemy lands. One condition under which such a system must function is that of concealment of the agent's point of origin. Hence the strategic techniques of employing brief, infrequent transmissions and rarely used frequencies. Another condition is that of guardedness, the object being to prevent the enemy from acquiring the message and the means being the use of some kind of code and cypher. A third condition is authentication. Here the object of the home office is to ensure that the person claiming to be the sender really is. (One solution here is familiarity with the transmission style of each individual agent.) A further condition is that the agent be able to keep his communication equipment in working order. Here the solution often has been to split the agent role in two, one man looking after what was to be transmitted and another man (by virtue of his training) looking after the transmitter.[56] Note, we deal here with the sociology of communication systems, namely the particular social conditions under which a particular kind of communication system must function.

Look now at one further social element of the communication system in question: what might be called the issue of "frame." Given a well-received, easily understandable message, what light is the message to be seen in, what systematic, word-by-word rereading is to be given it? Is the sender engaged in what he appears to be doing, namely, sending a serious, reliable message? Or is he merely practicing his sending, or engaging in a joke, or sending a false message because he is now working for the other side, or sending a message at the point of a gun, the message being designed by him to make this evident to the recipients?

In order to allow the intended recipient to deal with the frame of the message, intelligence communication systems sometimes employ what are called "security checks." The sender is required to preface each transmission with some otherwise meaningless sign which can be unapparently omitted from transmissions made under threat, thereby warning the home office to be wary of what it receives and what it sends. It is here that strategic analysis contributes to an understanding of communication systems, for security checks in practice apparently do not work out very well. There is the fact that those who receive messages in the home office have

[56] A division of role labor, incidentally, which coincides with the one between gentlemen and commoners, and between officers and enlisted men. During World War II, there was still a tendency to assume persons who could engage in the political aspects of intelligence work were not the sort who could spend the time learning to be adept at tinkering with the insides of wireless equipment.

to anticipate a certain amount of "noise" in the transmission; in addition, they have to assume that the sender will not always be careful to follow instructions regarding security checks.[57] In consequence, recipients tend to read the absence of a check as a sign of sloppiness, not capture. More to the point, there is the systematically produced problem that if the recipient shows, in any way, that the sender has succeeded in transmitting the warning, then this can endanger the life of the threatened agent and ruin the chances of feeding him false messages; yet if no sign is given that the warning has been noted, then the sender may feel obliged to increase the obviousness of the warning sign until those who are forcing him to transmit, themselves realize that he is trying to give the false show away.[58] Here, then, we have an example of how a mechanism in a communication system —security checks—can render the system unstable for strategic reasons.[59]

It is possible, then, to specify a communication system and to consider the strategic implications of its various conditions. Taking the same focus—a particular communication system —it is similarly possible to consider the bearing of social relationships and face-to-face interaction upon that system. In this way, various substantive areas can be drawn upon in a clear and subordinated way for what they can tell us about a communication system. But in practice, when the term *com-*

---

[57] E. Cookridge, *Inside S.O.E.* (London: Arthur Barker, 1966), pp. 420–421.

[58] See B. Sweet-Escott, *Baker Street Irregular* (London: Methuen, 1965), pp. 211–212.

[59] A whole series of these structural dilemmas exist. A further example: If field officers are to make best use of military intelligence sent from headquarters, the message transmitted should be quickly and accurately understandable, and this without the use of cumbersome equipment. On the other hand, if security and secrecy are to be maintained, elaborate decoding and deciphering techniques will have to be built in to the communication system. Clearly, the exigencies of battle make a strategic compromise necessary between speed and security.

munication is used, little clarity and consistency is found as to just what it is that is being investigated.

In this paper, of course, communication was not a central subject matter. Assessments were one central issue, it is true, but these assessments were as often a result of expression gleaned as they were a result of communications conveyed. Go back to our lion and note that even though he can perceive a movement to the tree, and even though Harry must decide on the value of this move by bearing in mind its visibility, still one deals here with assessment, not communication. Harry, in electing to dash for the tree, and doing so, is not communicating his move, as he would were he to phone home and tell his mother what course of action he has decided upon; he is simply making a move that has as one of its constitutive features the deplorable fact that evidence of its being under way will be readily available to the opposition, and the opposition is such as to make use of this information to worsen Harry's situation.

A similar point can be made if we turn back to board games that are played "for fun," that is, games where the intrinsic or game resources are not clearly linked to extrinsic ones and apparently must in themselves provide the motivation for play. For here it looks as though the players are merely engaged in signaling openly the moves that they make, that is, "communicating" their moves. But in fact, to speak of conveying a move on a board game is a loose way of describing what occurs.

In games for fun the parties must start with the shared sentiments that winning within the rules is desirable and significant—a condition not always satisfied, of course, as when Harry is obliged to play against someone much less skilled than himself. Once the world of the game has been jointly achieved, then a good or lucky move can become a meaningful gain.

Even here, however, a move is only incidentally a means

143

of communication, and it should not be surprising that some moves are invisible uncommunicated ones. The fact that little by way of enforcement machinery or extrinsic resources is required is not to be taken as a sign that pure or mere communication is involved in the moves, but rather as evidence that the *whole game* is cut off from the material world. The real problem of enforcement in fun-only games is not that of a commitment to a particular move made, but rather that of involvement in the world of the game; once this involvement is ensured, then the serious taking of moves follows. In such seriously engaged games, moves inform, but this is but one aspect of the move; what each move does, in fact, is to use up a choice made available in the game, and to use it up in a particular way that has implications for the value that the other players can then obtain by their moves. (Whereas, say, in exhibition chess, the play-by-play designation of moves on a large screen *does* involve mere communication.) In a game of strategy, the world is changed by each move, but in the case of fun-only games, this happens to be a world unseriously sustained by the joint involvement of the players; in fateful games, of course, it is the wider world that is involved.

There remains a final issue regarding the place of strategic interaction relative to other analytical frameworks in social psychology. This has to do with the difficult distinction between strategic interaction and what can be called "expression games."

At the beginning of the paper it was suggested that the two main moves open to Harry the hunted—bolting for the tree or "freezing"—raise the issue of visibility, and that, on this ground alone (although there are others), the two moves were radically different. Although this is the case, it is also the case that in the game between Harry and the lion a move is something in addition to a resource for assessment—it is an objective circumstances-altering action whose efficacy just happens to be influenced by the issue of visibility. Now the complication resides in the fact that if we are willing to fore-

144

go considering Harry's full plight and are willing to restrict ourselves to issues about visibility and invisibility we can, in fact, construct a little game out of these contingencies, a game wherein the whole value and character of a move has to do with assessment and its management. We can, in fact, abstract or excise from any occasion of strategic interaction an expression game. And this I have tried to do elsewhere.[60] But while this narrowing of focus is possible, we must here see that each of these expression games can properly be considered also as one component, and a variable one, of something more inclusive, a game concerning objective courses of action, an occasion of strategic interaction.

Let me repeat: In the analysis of strategic interaction, moves are central, but these constitute a class that is broader than the one derived from moves in expression games. During occasions of strategic interaction, a move consists of a structured course of action available to a player which, when taken, objectively alters the situation of the participants. Some of these moves are concealed, some visible; when visible, the question will always arise as to the reading that the opponent places on the event, namely the assessment he makes in terms of it. But this reading will be merely a contingency of the interaction, certainly not the whole thing. What is effected by strategic moves is not merely a state of information, but rather courses of action taken. Thus we can expect to find situations where Harry elects a course of action knowing that he thereby provides the other side with information they can use against him, but in spite of this cost finds that the other gains outweigh the price in information.[61]

---

[60] "Expression Games," this volume.
[61] Examples are provided by Jervis, *op. cit.*

STRATEGIC INTERACTION
Erving Goffman

"The broad topic is communication directed specifically to situations like espionage and to situations like international politics. . . . Goffman deals with the topic descriptively, draws on a wide variety of sources, and uses analogy to demonstrate, clarify, and explain"—*Choice*.

The two essays in this book deal with the calculative, gamelike aspects of interaction. Goffman examines the strategy of words and deeds; he uses the term "strategic interaction" to describe those gamelike events in which each player's situation is fully dependent on the move of his opponent and in which each player knows this and has the wit to use his awareness.

Expression games are always only a party of strategic interaction. The author uses vivid examples from espionage literature and high-level political maneuvers to show how men mislead each other in the information game.

In strategic interaction, the player's move is the central concern, and expression games are secondary, for as Goffman makes clear, often when it seems that a man's word sets off the action, the action has already been completed.

Those who gamble with their wits, and those who study those who do, will find this analysis important and stimulating.

The first volume in the Conduct and Communication Series.

Studio 1676
Designer Ron Shender

University of Pennsylvania Press
Blockley Hall, 418 Service Drive
Philadelphia, Pennsylvania 19104   ISBN 0-8122-1011-5